THE GOSPEL FOR MOVING TARGETS

THE GOSPEL FOR MOVING TARGETS

Helping Active Children Grow in Grace

NANCY SNYDER

Shepherd Press
Wapwallopen, Pennsylvania

The Gospel for Moving Targets

ISBN:
Print: 978-1-63342-109-7
Mobi: 978-1-63342-108-0
ePub: 978-1-63342-107-3

Published by **Shepherd Press**
P.O. Box 24
Wapwallopen,
Pennsylvania 18660

eBooks: www.shepherdpress.com/ebooks

Unless otherwise noted, all Scripture citations are from The Holy Bible, NIV 1984

BP 22 21 20 19 18 17 16 15

Library of Congress Control Number: 71NALC9NIVRI

Library of Congress Cataloging-in-Publication Data

Cover Design by Content & Communication
Design and Typesetting by **documen** www.documen.co.uk
Printed in the United States of America

To Chuck

Little did you know, when you read and reread every letter during our long-distance courtship, that you would spend our marriage reading and rereading every word I write.

Your thousandfold love underlies each word.

Contents

——— *Unit 4: The Heart*

Lesson

Section 2: Transformed

Lesson

Section 3: Attention

Section 4: Pictures to Show

Section 5: Pictures to Download

Acknowledgments

I am indebted to those who prayed this project to fruition—Ann, Joanne, Janice, Traci, Linda, Jack, Cath, Julie, Ellen, Rose Marie, Lou, Lynn, Tree, Tom, and Lisa. Special thanks to Brad Bigney, Jerry Bridges, Sinclair Ferguson, Rose Marie Miller, Angela Watson, and Steve Viars for their gracious support. Heartfelt gratitude to Chuck Snyder for strong and tender involvement during each step of this project. Many thanks to Bola, Aimee, and Kauna Adebisi of Inner Hub Productions for capturing my vision on film, to Logos Academy for staging it (especially Jonathan, Gladys, and Heidi), and to these students for making it shine: Aja, Amani, Imagine, and Madison.

If not for God's grace, I would have no hope to share. If Rose Marie Miller and Rosann Trott had not taught me the riches of the gospel, I could not have written this book. If God had not blessed Chuck and me with Noah (who set our family spinning with wonder), Jesse (by whose days we could set our hearts), Joel (who made our home a waltzing whirligig), and AJ (who kept things humming and drumming), I would not have written this book. If I were not part of the vibrant learning community at Logos Academy, where students and staff sparkle with the glory of God, these lessons would never have been committed to paper. If not for Chuck's abounding encouragement, these lessons would have stayed in my classroom. If not for the hope-filled confidence of Cindy Kalinoski, the writing would have stayed on my computer. If not for Richard Riggall paving the way and prompting the first foundational lessons, this would not have been published. If not for the skillful team at Shepherd Press—Margy Tripp, who offered invaluable suggestions; Linda Riggall, who provided wise direction; Richard and Bonnie Irvin, who brought order with patience and skill; Caleb Irvin who revised and perfected several illustrations; Aaron Tripp and Thomas Wiley, who rounded out the shepherding team—no one would want to muddle through the mess. But, God did, and they did, so I did, and here it is—a gift of God's might and mercy.

Introduction

These hands-on devotional lessons are designed for children who struggle to sit still, keep quiet, pay attention, follow directions, or control their emotions. These lessons are also designed to help parents and teachers who love such children to aim the gospel at the hearts of moving targets.

The lessons are divided into three major sections which each emphasize one aspect of the growth process outlined in Ephesians 4:22–24.

"You were taught, with regard to your former way of life, *to put off your old self*, which is being corrupted by its deceitful desires; *to be made new in the attitude of your minds*; and *to put on the new self*, created to be like God in true righteousness and holiness." (Italics added).

Section 1: *Dealing with Feelings*. These lessons are designed to help children put off expressing and responding to emotions in sinful ways. This part of the devotional helps children clear the debris that blocks the gospel.

Section 2: *Transformed*. These activities are designed to help children renew their minds as they apply the gospel. The truths presented in these crucial lessons are repeated throughout the rest of the book to allow further opportunity for the Holy Spirit to teach.

Section 3: *Attention!* These lessons are designed to help children put on new actions and attitudes, since new people do new things.

Section 4 contains Pictures 1 to 14 that are to be shown directly to the children.

Section 5 contains miniatures of Pictures 15 to 37 that can be downloaded for printing and giving to the children from: www.shepherdpress.com/moving-targets

May God help you—parents and teachers who love rambunctious children—to put off everything that keeps you from loving these little ones, renew your thinking as you point children to the gospel of grace, and put on the character of Christ who blessed the children.

Section 1

Dealing With Feelings

Dealing With Feelings

It was God's idea to make us people with feelings. Adam and Eve experienced perfect emotions for the glory of God. Since the Fall, sin has ravaged our emotions. Jesus came to earth and honored God with every emotional nuance in every moment of his life. Jesus is not only our model for God-glorifying emotions, Jesus is our power for God-glorifying emotions.

Children who throw desks when they are angry or wail uncontrollably when they cannot find the gold crayon are misusing the God-given gift of emotions. The goal is not to put off feelings, for that would leave the children unable to know, trust, honor, love, and obey God. The goal is to put off sinful expressions of, and responses to, those feelings. The goal is not to ignore emotions, the goal is to dig under those emotions to see what buried treasure lies below, repent of misplaced treasure, and joyfully treasure Christ.

May God use these lessons to help you and the children you love express emotions humbly, know peace, and bolster hope:

My heart is not proud, O Lord
my eyes are not haughty;
I do not concern myself with great matters
or things too wonderful for me.
But I have stilled and quieted my soul;
like a weaned child with its mother,
like a weaned child is my soul within me.
O Israel, put your hope in the Lord
both now and forevermore.

Psalm 131

Teaching Tips

Any of these lessons can be divided into shorter mini-lessons to accommodate individual attention spans. Lessons are grouped into units. To most effectively teach the lessons, preview the entire unit before teaching any of its individual lessons. Save all materials created or taken from the appendix; many of these materials will be used in later lessons.

Lesson 1

In the Beginning, God

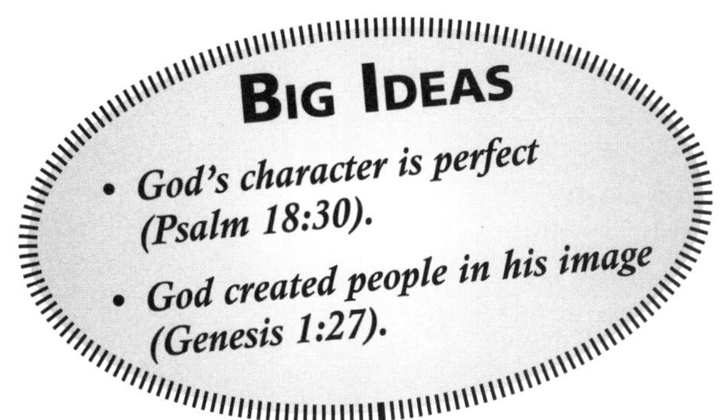

Big Ideas
• God's character is perfect (Psalm 18:30).
• God created people in his image (Genesis 1:27).

Materials

- Bible
- 1 piece of poster board
- Tape and Scissors
- 8.5 x 11 inch paper
- Adhesive labels or paper strips and glue
- Pencil or marker
- Optional: plants (living, artificial, or illustrated); animals (living, toy, or illustrated), snacks; activities

Activity:

1. Praise God that he is perfect. Ask God to help the children learn about and love him.
2. Read the first few words of Genesis 1:1. Explain that God has always been perfect in every way. Discuss God's character[1] by reading the following passages:

   God is good: Psalm 25:8a.
   God is righteous: Psalm 145:17.
   God is holy: Isaiah 6:3.
3. Read Psalm 36:5–6. Explain that God's character is so great that the Bible compares it to a lofty mountain. Tape the poster board into a cone shape and trim it so it looks and stands like a large mountain.
4. Read Genesis 1:27–28 and Genesis 2:15–25. Explain that God created people to reflect his image.
5. Tape the paper into a cone shape and trim it so it looks and stands like a small mountain. Discuss

Notes

1 God has many attributes that all exist in perfect unity. These three were chosen because God's goodness includes his love, kindness, mercy, patience, and grace. God's righteousness is the foundation of his justice and wrath. Every attribute of God is holy—morally perfect. God's love, kindness, mercy, and patience are holy; God's righteousness, justice, and wrath are holy.

NOTES

ways the smaller paper mountain reflects the image of the larger poster board mountain. For example, the paper mountain and the poster board mountain have similar shapes. Although the paper mountain is smaller and weaker (and may be a different color), it is something like the poster board mountain.

6. Write the words "good," "righteous," and "holy" on adhesive labels or strips of paper. Apply or glue the labels on the larger, poster board mountain as you discuss God's perfections. Everything God has ever thought, said, or done has been perfectly good, righteous, and holy.

7. Explain that, as the smaller paper mountain reflects the image of the larger poster board mountain, God made Adam and Eve to reflect his image. Write the words "good," "righteous," and "holy" on adhesive labels or strips of paper. As you discuss ways Adam and Eve reflected the image of God, tape the labels for those characteristics on the paper mountain.
   a. When Adam and Eve exercised dominion over the earth (Genesis 1:26) by working the garden and ruling over creation, they reflected the goodness of God (who is a good ruler over the earth).
   b. When Adam worked and guarded the garden (Genesis 2:15–17), he reflected the goodness, righteousness, and holiness of God.
   c. When Eve helped Adam (Genesis 2:18), she reflected the goodness of God (who provided her to be a helper for Adam).
   d. When Adam and Eve loved each other (Genesis 2:24), they reflected the goodness of the God who loved them.
   e. When Adam and Eve obeyed God (Genesis 2:16–17), they reflected the righteousness of God.
   f. When Adam and Eve refused to take the fruit of the one forbidden tree (Genesis 2:16–17), they reflected the holiness of God.

8. Save the poster board and paper mountains to use in later lessons.

9. Praise God for his goodness, righteousness, and holiness.

Options:

1. Design a space that models Eden.

2. Fill it with plants (living, artificial, or illustrated) and animals (living, toy, or illustrated).

3. Display tantalizing snacks (taped to a picture of a tree or hanging on a tree branch "planted" in a bucket).

4. Instruct the children not to eat those snacks. Give the children enjoyable activities to do in that space—drawing animals and naming them, creating things with clay, eating delicious fruits and vegetables, etc.

5. Emphasize that this is a holy place where no sin should ever occur.

Review:

When the children do something that reflects God's character, thank God for the ways they reflect God's image.

Notes

Lesson 2

The Fall and Falling Short

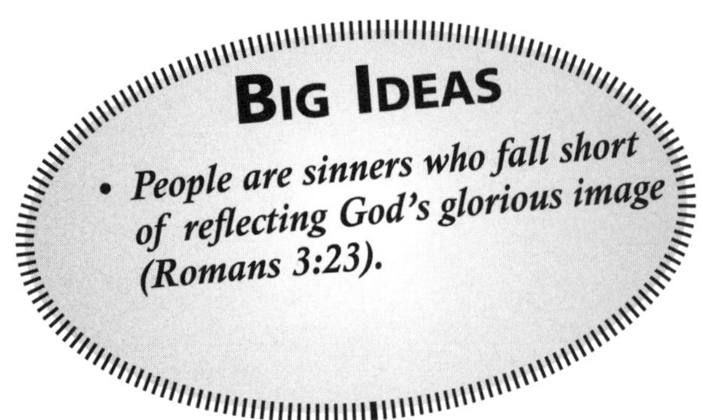

Big Ideas
• People are sinners who fall short of reflecting God's glorious image (Romans 3:23).

Materials

- Bible
- Paper mountain (the smaller mountain made in Lesson 1) (After disfiguring the mountain in this lesson, keep it for Lesson 11.)

Activity:

1. Praise God that his righteousness is greater than a high mountain. Ask God to help the children reflect his image.

2. Read Genesis 3:1–19, emphasizing the sad truth that Adam and Eve did not follow God's good, righteous, and holy way, but followed the wrong way by disobeying God. Let the children tear the labels off the paper mountain, disfiguring (and possibly tearing) the mountain, as sin disfigured the image of God in people.

3. Contrast God's perfection with people's sinfulness:

   a. Everything God has ever thought is good, righteous, and holy. Eve thought that, if she ate the fruit, she would be like God (Genesis 3:5–6).

   b. Everything God has ever desired is good, righteous, and holy. Adam and Eve sinned by desiring the fruit more than they desired God (Genesis 3:6).

   c. Everything God has ever felt is good, righteous, and holy, but Adam and Eve felt like rebelling, instead of feeling a holy fear of disobeying God (Genesis 3:6).

   d. Everything God has ever done has come from his perfect character. When Adam and Eve

Notes

disobeyed God, they, and all who came after them, were no longer good (Romans 3:12). They, and all who came after them, were no longer righteous (Romans 3:10). They, and all who came after them, were no longer holy (Romans 3:18, 23). From that moment on, all people have sinned in their thoughts, desires, feelings, and actions.

4. Confess specific ways each of you has fallen short of God's glory (Romans 3:23) and failed to reflect his glorious image. Model for the children as you ask God to forgive you for sinful thoughts (worrying thoughts that doubt God's goodness, for example), sinful desires (such as wanting to control everything rather than trusting God), sinful feelings (feeling angry about having to wait, for example), and actions (such as yelling because some piece of technology is not working).

5. Read Genesis 3:15–24. Discuss ways this passage shows God's goodness, righteousness, and holiness:

   a. God is so good he promised that Eve would have children and one of her descendants would save people from their sin (Genesis 3:15, 20).

   b. God is so righteous he punished sin (Genesis 3:16–19).

   c. God is so holy he drove sinful people away from the holy place where he had dwelled with them in the Garden of Eden (Genesis 3:23–24).

6. Read 2 Corinthians 5:21. Explain that, when Jesus lived on earth, he was good, righteous, and holy. He was not simply like God (as the paper mountain is something like the poster board mountain); he was God. Everything he thought, said, felt, and did was good, righteous, and holy. Explain that Jesus became like us so he could save us. Marvel that Jesus Christ could remain God and yet become human. On the cross, Jesus took the sin of all who believe in him. He became sin. Jesus was the only one who perfectly reflected the image of God, but he died for people who

Notes

have disfigured his image by their sin. People who believe in Jesus are made new. As new people, Christians work in partnership with God to become more like God. When God brings his children to heaven, they reflect his image without any sin.

7. Thank God that Jesus became like us, so we could become like him. Ask God to make each of you more like Christ.

Notes

Options:

1. If you created a model of Eden after Lesson 1, let the children enjoy it until they disobey in it (either by eating the forbidden snack or by treating one another sinfully).
2. At that time, dismantle that sacred space and explain that God, in his goodness, righteousness, and holiness, guarded the path to the tree of life so that people would not live forever in their sinful misery.
3. Then teach this lesson.

Review:

1. When the children do something that does not reflect God's character, talk about the ways they failed to reflect God's glorious image.
2. Help them confess specific ways they failed to reflect God's character and ask for his forgiveness.
3. Encourage them to believe that God has the power to make them like Christ.

Lesson 3

The Engine and the Engineer

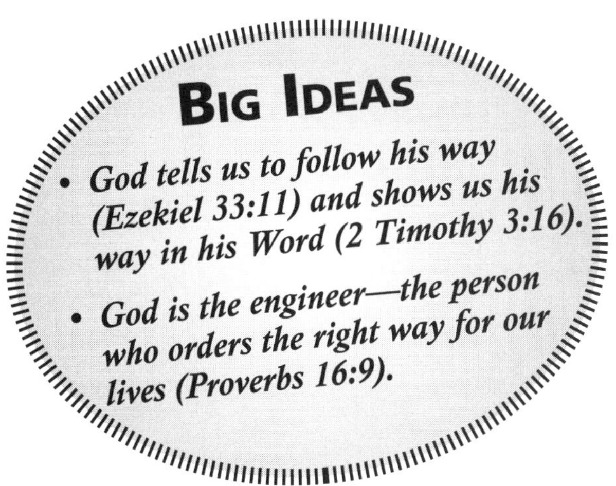

Big Ideas
• God tells us to follow his way (Ezekiel 33:11) and shows us his way in his Word (2 Timothy 3:16).
• God is the engineer—the person who orders the right way for our lives (Proverbs 16:9).

Materials

- Bible
- Train set or download Picture-15 *Train Engine* (see page 287), and homemade track
- Optional: glue and cardboard; if using the picture of the train, the picture may be glued to cardboard to make it durable for frequent reuse
- Paper on which you have written "God's way"

Activity:

1. Thank God for being the good ruler who directs our lives. Thank Jesus for being the strong person who gives us power to follow his way.

2. Review Lesson 2 by explaining that, because of sin, we all follow the wrong way. Because of his goodness, righteousness, and holiness, God tells us to turn from the wrong way and follow his way (Ezekiel 33:11).

3. Tell the children that God shows us his way in his Word. From 2 Timothy 3:16, explain that the Bible is useful for teaching us who God is and how to follow his way. This verse also explains that Scripture is useful for correcting us when we have not followed God's way and getting us back to God's way when we have gone astray.

4. Build a long track from the toy train set or mark a route for a homemade train track. Place paper on which you wrote "God's way" next to the track. Explain that God shows us his way in the Bible. God is the engineer (Proverbs 16:9) who orders the right way for our lives.

Notes

5. Read Psalm 119:112. Explain that following God's statutes or decrees means doing things his way. Just as the train follows the track to the very end, we want to follow God's Word and his way to the very end of our lives.

6. If using a train set, have the children run the engine on the track while repeating Psalm 119:112. If using the Picture-15 *Train Engine* (see page 287), have the children move it along the route they created (as if the train is moving on a long track) while reciting the verse.

7. Ask God to help the children set their hearts on keeping his Word to the end of their lives.

Notes

Options:

The children who are waiting for turns with the train can lower crossbars by using their hands or a crossbar from the train set. This helps the children who are waiting for turns to be patient. The child who is pushing the train along the track has increased opportunities to practice self-control (while waiting for a crossbar to be raised, for example). This gives the children opportunities to practice doing things God's way (rather than doing things their own way).

Review:

There will be many natural opportunities to review this lesson when the children sin. Help them see how they departed from God's way. Ask God to give them a desire to follow God and his way.

Lesson 4

Don't Crash!

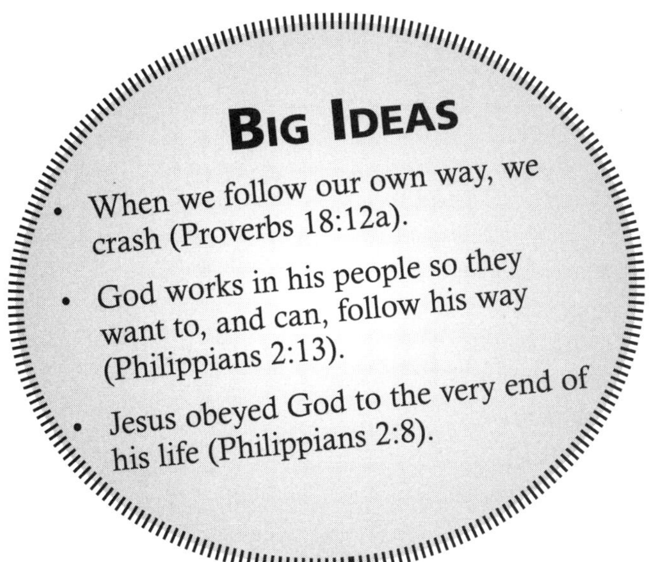

Big Ideas
• When we follow our own way, we crash (Proverbs 18:12a).
• God works in his people so they want to, and can, follow his way (Philippians 2:13).
• Jesus obeyed God to the very end of his life (Philippians 2:8).

Materials

- Bible
- Table or desk
- Train set or download Picture-15 *Train Engine* (see page 287), and homemade track (from Lesson 3)
- Paper on which you have written the words "My Way"

Notes

Activity:

1. Ask God to help the children set their hearts on keeping God's Word to the very end.

2. Explain that following our own way means trying to make ourselves the engineers who direct our lives. People who follow their own way do what they feel like doing even if it is disobedient to God. Following our own way, instead of following God's way, is sin. Confess instances of following our own way. Examples follow, but feel free to substitute the sins your children struggle with:

   a. Grabbing a toy from another child, instead of waiting for a turn.

   b. Sneakily feeding your vegetables to the dog, instead of gratefully eating them.

3. Read Proverbs 18:12a. Explain that when we follow our own way, instead of following God's way, we are being proud. When we proudly follow our own way, things go wrong and we crash.

4. On top of the table or desk, build a track using the toy train set or mark a route for a homemade train track. Make the track stop at the edge of the table or desk. Label the track with the words "My Way."

5. With the other children watching from a safe distance, give each child a turn to recite Proverbs 18:12a while pushing the engine along the track until it crashes over the edge.

6. Read Philippians 2:13. Ask the children if they always feel like obeying God. Acknowledge that we all struggle with wanting our own way sometimes. Explain that God has power to enable us to want to follow his way and to obey with joy. As we believe in God's power, we can joyfully obey him.[2]

7. Read Philippians 2:8. Explain that Jesus followed God's way to the end of his life and took the terrible crash we deserve for following our own way. Call the children to trust this glorious Savior.

8. Thank God that, because of what Jesus did, everyone who believes in him can follow God's way. Ask God to help the children follow his way to the very end (Psalm 119:112).

Options:

1. Scripture has many examples of people who followed their own way and crashed.

2. According to 1 Corinthians 10:6 and 11, these things were written down to warn us not to follow our own way.

3. Extend this lesson by discussing some of these accounts.

4. Read Matthew 10:39.

Notes

2 The Spirit's power to transform lives through the gospel is thoroughly addressed in Section 2 of this devotional.

5. Explain that people who try to find their lives by following their own way end up losing their lives.

6. If God's Word says to do something we don't feel like doing, losing our lives means asking God to help us obey, believing God can help us obey with joy, then happily doing so. Jesus did not feel like dying on the cross, but asked God to help him obey, believed God would help him obey, and obeyed for the joy set before him (Hebrews 12:2), so we could find our lives in him. Those who give up their lives by bringing their thoughts, words, feelings, and actions in line with God's Word will live forever with Christ.

Review:

1. When the children have emotional upsets, ask if they have been following the track of God's way or their own way.

2. Discuss the track the children followed and help them understand what fueled their crash.

3. After such self-evaluation, help them confess their sin to God.

4. Explain the hope of trusting in Christ, who always followed God's way and died to take the punishment for those who proudly follow their own way.

5. Pray that God would give them his power to joyfully follow God's way.

Notes

Lesson 5

Twists, Turns, and Tunnels

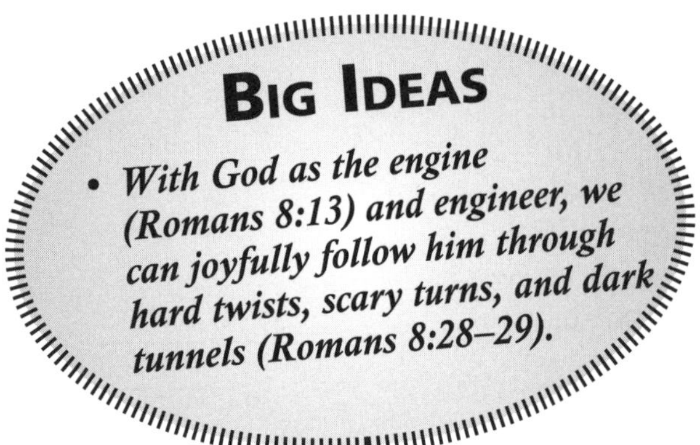

Big Ideas
• With God as the engine (Romans 8:13) and engineer, we can joyfully follow him through hard twists, scary turns, and dark tunnels (Romans 8:28–29).

Materials

- Bible
- Train set or download Picture-15 *Train Engine* (see page 287), and homemade track (from Lessons 3 and 4)

Activity:

1. Thank God that Jesus always trusted his Father as he perfectly followed God through all the hard twists, scary turns, and dark tunnels of his life—including dying on the cross. Ask God to help the children believe in Christ and follow God's way to the very end (Psalm 119:112).

2. Discuss some of the twists, turns, and tunnels in the children's lives, such as:

    a. Not being called on when they want to give an answer.

    b. Not being picked to do something special.

    c. Having to share their favorite toys.

    d. Getting sick.

    e. Being blamed for something they did not do.

    f. Losing a loved one.

3. Whether using a train set or a homemade obstacle course, make a very complex track. As children take turns running the train around the track, explain that—no matter how many twists, turns, and tunnels they face each day—God can give them joy as they obey God by following his way.

Notes

4. Read Romans 8:13. Explain that God the Spirit is the powerful engine who enables us to follow God's way.

5. From Romans 8:28–29 (ESV), explain that God is a wise and good engineer who designs the tracks of our lives so that "all things work together for good" for those who follow God's way. That means the hard twists, scary turns, and dark tunnels are all part of the good track God has planned for our lives. Further explain that the good purpose all the hard things work toward is conforming God's children "to the image of his Son." So, God uses all the hard things in our lives to make us like Jesus.

6. Have the children recite Psalm 119:32 as they move the train along the track.

7. Remind the children that Jesus always obeyed God (Philippians 2:8). Encourage them to believe God and hope in his promise to work so that the children want to, and do, follow God's way (Philippians 2:13).

8. Ask God to set the children free to run in the path of his commands. Pray that God would give them joy as they follow his way through all the twists, turns, and tunnels of their lives.

Options:

1. Whether using a train set or a homemade course, the children who are waiting for turns can put obstacles along the track by lowering crossbars, raising drawbridges, etc. This will engage the children who are waiting for turns while encouraging patience in the children who are running the train.

2. Children who studied Matthew 10:39 in Lesson 4 may be reminded that Jesus gave up his life so they could find their lives in Jesus.

Notes

3. Assure them of God's promise that, if they give up their lives by bringing their feelings in line with God's Word, they will find lives of joy.

Notes

Review:

When the children face difficulties, remind them that God is the engineer who designs the course of their lives. He is also the engine who can give them power to joyfully follow him through all the twists, turns, and tunnels of their lives.

Lesson 6

Energy Is a Gift from God

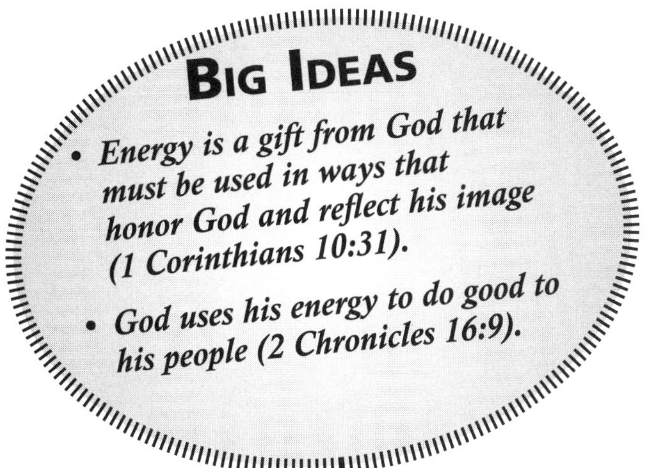

Big Ideas
• Energy is a gift from God that must be used in ways that honor God and reflect his image (1 Corinthians 10:31).
• God uses his energy to do good to his people (2 Chronicles 16:9).

Materials

- Bible
- Picture-1 *Traffic Light* on page 257
- Whiteboard or paper, and markers
- Train set or picture of a train (from previous lessons) and homemade track

Activity:

1. Ask God to help the children put all their energy into honoring him.
2. Ask the children what energy is. Highlight responses that include the ability (or desire) to do something.
3. Review the perfection of God's character (from Lesson 1) and point out that God always uses his energy in ways that are good, righteous, and holy.
4. Read Acts 17:28; explain that we have energy because God has energy (Isaiah 40:28). God gives us energy to live and move. Read 1 Corinthians 10:31. Help the children see that, as they must use the gift of food to honor God and reflect his image, they must use all God's gifts to glorify him. Explain that energy is a gift from God that must be used in ways that are good, righteous, and holy.

Notes

5. Brainstorm ways of using the gift of energy to honor God and reflect his image (Romans 12:1):
   a. Loving, enjoying, and praising God.
   b. Running joyfully at playtime.
   c. Talking kindly with friends during playtime.
   d. Helping someone who has a need.
   e. Putting energy into keeping still and quiet when told to do so.
6. Confess ways each of you has misused the gift of energy to disobey God. Examples follow:
   a. Thinking about video games during worship.
   b. Running in the hall at school or in the sanctuary during worship.
   c. Talking with friends when told to listen to the teacher at school or church.
   d. Being mean to a brother or sister.
   e. Disrupting people during worship or class.
7. Show Picture-1 *Traffic Light* on page 257. Explain that the traffic light uses energy to produce its red or green light. In the same way, the children use the gift of energy when they have a green light (to go ahead and play or talk) and when they have a red light (to keep their bodies still and their mouths closed).

8. Have the children line up at a whiteboard or give them paper and markers. Explain that they can only draw and color when you say, "Energy green light." When you say, "Energy red light," they should put their energy into stopping all talk and movement. Pray for and encourage the children who struggle to quiet themselves for the "Energy red light." Play this game as time and interest allow.

9. Read 2 Chronicles 16:9. Even though Jesus always used his energy to perfectly obey God (so was blameless), Jesus took the punishment for the sinful ways that people who believe in him have misused the gift of energy. God hates sin, so he

Notes

turned away from Jesus, took away his support, and poured out his wrath against sin. Because Jesus took the punishment for our sins, God uses his energy to support (lovingly help) his children.

10. Praise God that he uses his energy to support his children. Ask God to help the children use his gift of energy to honor God and reflect his image.

Options:

11. Before announcing a transition (such as the end of playtime), give the children a yellow light by telling them they have a few minutes to prepare for the transition. Pray for the children and remind them that energy is a gift from God that must be used the way he says. Teach them that life is like an energy game in which we put all the energy God gives us into honoring him and reflecting his image.

12. The energy game from Step 8 may be played with other activities, such as running in place.

Review:

1. Use the train track to review. As the children move the train around the track, talk about using the gift of energy to follow God through all the twists, turns, tunnels, and red lights God has planned for their lives.

2. As problems arise on the tracks of their lives, encourage the children to use the gift of energy to honor God and reflect his image.

Notes

Lesson 7

Energy to Know, Trust, Honor, Love, and Obey

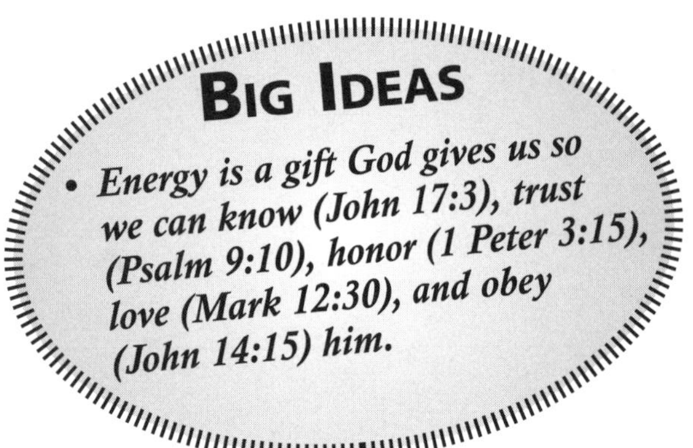

Big Ideas
• Energy is a gift God gives us so we can know (John 17:3), trust (Psalm 9:10), honor (1 Peter 3:15), love (Mark 12:30), and obey (John 14:15) him.

Materials

- Bible
- Optional: materials for energy game

Notes

Activity:

1. Thank God for the energy he has given the children. Ask God to help them use the gift of energy to know, trust, honor, love, and obey God.

2. Ask the children to listen for what God calls them to do in these verses: John 17:3, Psalm 9:10, 1 Peter 3:15, Mark 12:30, and John 14:15. Explain that energy is a gift God gives us so we can know, trust, honor, love, and obey God.

3. Read or retell the account of God saving Noah's family. It will take approximately five minutes to read Genesis 6:11–22, 7:6–10, 7:17–21, 7:24–8:5, 8:13–14, 8:18–9:3, and 9:8–15.

4. Discuss ways Noah used the energy God gave him to know, trust, love, honor, and obey God. Examples follow:

   a. Listening carefully to God's instructions (Genesis 6:14–21).

   b. Building the ark and covering it with pitch so it would float (Genesis 6:14, 22).

   c. Paying careful attention to the exact measurements of the ark (Genesis 6:15, 22).

NOTES

d. Gathering and storing food in the ark (Genesis 6:21, 22).

e. Building an altar and worshiping God (Genesis 8:20).

5. Discuss what could have happened if Noah had not used the energy God gave him to obey by building the ark.

6. Discuss how Noah would have grown in his knowledge of God as he used his energy to know (and love) God:

   a. When he saw God judge sin, Noah knew God's holiness and righteousness (Genesis 6:11–13; 7:21).

   b. When God entered into covenant with Noah to save him and his family, Noah knew God's mercy (Genesis 6:18).

   c. When he saw the mighty waters, Noah knew God's power (Genesis 7:17–20).

   d. When the ark rested on dry land, Noah knew God's kindness (Genesis 8:1–5).

   e. When God saved animals (Genesis 7:8) for people to eat (9:3) and sacrifice for worship and atonement for sin (8:20–21; Leviticus 1:3–17), Noah knew God's holiness and wisdom.

   f. When God covenanted never again to destroy the earth by flood (Genesis 8:21–22; 9:8–15), Noah knew God's love and faithfulness.

7. As the ark covered and protected Noah and his family from God's judgment, Christ's righteousness covers and protects Christians from God's judgment (Romans 4:7–8). As Noah and his family found refuge in the ark, God's people find refuge in him (Hebrews 6:18–20).

8. Thank God that Jesus used his energy to cover his people from God's judgment. Ask God to help the children use their energy to know, trust, honor, love, and obey God.

Options:

Notes

Before the children listen to the Bible story (in Step 3), play the energy game (as described in Step 8 of Lesson 6). After giving the children time to move freely then quiet themselves, encourage engaged listening by guiding the children to act out the account as you read it.

Review:

Every circumstance provides an opportunity to use the gift of energy to know, trust, honor, love, and obey God. Help the children recognize opportunities for knowing, trusting, honoring, and loving God's attributes.

Lesson 8

All His Energy Working in Me

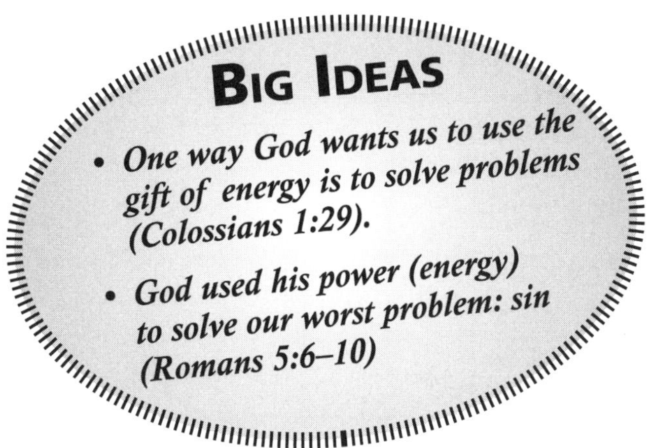

Big Ideas
• One way God wants us to use the gift of energy is to solve problems (Colossians 1:29).
• God used his power (energy) to solve our worst problem: sin (Romans 5:6–10)

Materials

- Bible
- Picture-2 *Lighthouse* on page 259
- Picture-3 *Construction Workers* on page 261
- Materials for energy game
- Optional: train set or picture of a train (from previous lessons) and homemade track

Activity:

1. Thank God for the energy he has given the children. Ask God to help them use the gift of energy to solve problems in ways that honor God and reflect his image.

2. Explain that one of the reasons God gives people energy is so they can solve problems. Show Picture-2 *Lighthouse* on page 259 and Picture-3 *Construction Workers* on page 261; discuss ways energy is being used to solve problems.

   a. A lighthouse uses the energy of light to solve the problem of ships crashing.

   b. Construction workers use the energy of motion as they build homes and solve the problem of people being cold and wet.

3. Play the energy game (as described in Step 8 of Lesson 6) to give the children an outlet for their energy. Then tell the children to put all their energy into keeping their bodies still and learning how God used his energy (power) to solve our worst problem: sin (following our own way, instead of following God's way).

Notes

Notes

4. Read Romans 5:6, 8. Explain that God is so good, righteous, and holy that he hates sin and must punish sinners. Explain that we have no energy or power to solve the problem of our sin. God the Father used his energy (power) to plan a way to save sinners while remaining just and holy himself. God the Son used his energy to obey the Father perfectly and take the punishment for sinners who believe in him, so they can be right with God. God the Spirit uses his energy to give people new life.

5. Read Ephesians 1:19–20. Explain that God's power—the same power that raised Jesus from the dead—now works in people who believe in Jesus, so God's energy in them can love God, love others, and solve problems in ways that honor God and reflect his image.

6. Read Colossians 1:29; explain that God's energy worked through Paul to solve the problem of people's sin as Paul taught them about salvation through Christ.

7. Brainstorm ways of using God's gift of energy to know God and help others know him (Colossians 1:28).

8. Thank God that he solved the problem of our sin by sending Jesus—who used all his energy to honor God, love people, and solve our worst problem. Ask God to help the children use the gift of energy to love God, love others, and solve problems. Call the children to trust in Christ.

Options:

Notes

1. Whether using a train set or homemade track, make a complex track and have the children push the train along the track. As problems arise on the train track (broken track, stuck drawbridge, etc.) or the track of the children's lives, teach the children to put the gift of energy into solving problems in ways that honor God.

2. Set aside time to carry out some of the ideas you brainstormed (in Step 7) for using God's gift of energy to know God and help others know him.

Review:

Every conflict or challenge provides an opportunity to use the gift of energy to solve problems. Pray through each problem and guide the children in ways of using the gift of energy to solve these problems in ways that honor God (Proverbs 3:5, 6).

Lesson 9

Energy Solutions

Big Ideas

- *People can foolishly use the energy God gives them to dishonor God, do evil toward others, and make their problems worse (Genesis 37:3–32).*
- *People can wisely use the energy God gives them to love God, love people, and solve problems in ways that honor God (Genesis 41).*

Materials

- Bible

Notes

Activity:

1. Ask God to help the children use the gift of energy in ways that honor God and reflect his glorious image.

2. Read Genesis 37:3–11. Discuss the problems Joseph's brothers faced:

   a. Their father's favoritism toward Joseph (Genesis 37:3).

   b. Their feelings of hatred and jealousy (Genesis 37:4, 11).

   c. Joseph's talk about his dreams (Genesis 37:5–10).

3. Think of ways Joseph's brothers could have used energy wisely to do good and solve their problems:

   a. Confessing their hatred and asking God's forgiveness.

   b. Asking God to help them honor their father and love their brother, then doing loving acts.

4. Read Genesis 37:12–32. Discuss the foolish (sinful) ways Joseph's brothers used energy to

dishonor God, do evil to others, and make their problems worse:

a. They planned to kill Joseph (Genesis 37:18).

b. They planned to hide their sin and deceive their father (Genesis 37:20).

c. They decided to sell Joseph as a slave (Genesis 37:26–27).

d. They carried out their plan to hide their sin and deceive their father (Genesis 37:31–32).

5. Explain that Joseph suffered many things. Later, God made Joseph a leader in Egypt. During years when the harvest was plentiful, Joseph stored food for the coming drought (Genesis 41:33–40). Eventually Joseph's brothers came to Egypt seeking food from Joseph. Read Genesis 42:19–38 and discuss ways the brothers' sinful solutions to their problem of hating Joseph made their problems worse:

   a. They carried guilt all those years (Genesis 42:21).

   b. They thought they were being punished because of their sin (Genesis 42:22).

   c. Simeon had to stay imprisoned in Egypt (Genesis 42:19, 24).

   d. They made their father's grief worse (Genesis 42:38).

6. Read Genesis 41. Discuss ways Joseph wisely used energy to love God, love people, and solve problems in ways that honored God.

   a. Joseph loved and honored God by saying God could interpret dreams (Genesis 41:16). Joseph honored God by believing God would reveal the dream's meaning, then explaining it (41:25–32).

   b. Joseph wisely used the energy God gave him to love people and solve problems by explaining how Pharaoh could save the Egyptians from death (41:33–36).

Notes

c. For seven years, Joseph wisely used the energy God gave him to love people and solve problems as he supervised the gathering and storing of surplus food (Genesis 41:48–49).

d. For seven years, Joseph wisely used the energy God gave him to love people and solve problems as he supervised the sale of food to Egyptians and people from other countries (Genesis 41:56–57).

7. Read Matthew 26:14–16. As Joseph was sold for silver coins, Christ was also sold for silver coins. Even though he was a sinner, Joseph's life was spared. Christ, even though he was perfectly obedient to God, took the punishment we deserve for using the energy God gives in ways that dishonor him.

8. Thank God that Jesus used his energy to honor God as he solved the problem of our sin.

Options:

Many children's books feature people wisely or foolishly using the gift of energy to solve problems. Extend this lesson by reading and discussing some of those books.

Review:

When the children complicate their lives through unbiblical solutions to problems (such as hitting a child who is being mean to them), help them ask for forgiveness from God and others. Help the children think of ways they could have used God's gift of energy to solve the problem in ways that honor God.

Notes

Lesson 10

Feelings Are Gifts from God

Big Ideas

- ***Feelings are gifts from God (James 1:17) that should be used to know, trust, honor, love, and obey God, love others, and solve problems.***
- ***Because the Holy Spirit lives in people who believe in Jesus, they can use the energy generated by feelings in ways that honor God, love others, and solve problems (John 14:15–16).***

Materials

- Bible
- Small squares of card stock or heavy paper
- Crayons or markers
- Decorative box
- Optional: emoticons printed from the Internet

Notes

Activity:

1. Ask God to help the children honor him with their feelings.
2. On the squares of paper, have the children draw faces that reflect different emotions.
3. As the children are drawing, have them take turns naming the feelings they are representing and recalling times when they felt those emotions.
4. Put the pictures in the decorative box. Read James 1:17 and discuss ways in which feelings are good gifts from God that help us know, trust, honor, love, and obey God, love others, and solve problems.
    a. *Happiness*: How does happy obedience honor God as our delight?
    b. *Fear*: How does fear keep us from things God wants to protect us from—sin, running in front of cars, and disobeying authorities?

NOTES

c. *Anger*: How does anger motivate us to protect someone who is being hurt by another person?

d. *Compassion*: How does compassion motivate us to love people who are lonely, afraid, or misunderstood?

e. *Sadness*: How does sadness motivate us to change a situation?

5. Discuss and confess sinful ways of misusing feelings:

   a. *Happiness*: Demanding what we think will make us happy, rather than entrusting our desires to God, is sinful (James 4:1–2).

   b. *Fear*: Responding to circumstances by worrying is sinful; worry does not honor God and reflect how wise and good he is in caring for his children (Philippians 4:6).

   c. *Anger*: Responding to circumstances by yelling at people is sinful because it does not honor and trust the God who judges all things rightly (Matthew 5:21–22).

   d. *Compassion*: Being so upset about someone's suffering that we are angry with God does not honor God as the one who is good and righteous in all he does. (See 1 Chronicles 13:5–11 for an example.)

   e. *Sadness*: It is sinful to respond to sad circumstances by treasuring what we lost more than we treasure God (2 Corinthians 7:29–31).

6. Tell the children that, when we bring our feelings in line with God's Word, the energy generated by those feelings can help us honor God, love others, and solve problems. Discuss examples:

   a. If we are happy under God's authority, the energy generated by happiness can help us find wise solutions to problems, rather than rushing into foolish solutions.

   b. If we fear sin's destructive power, the energy generated by fear can help us overcome temptation.

c. If we are angry because a bully is hurting a younger child, the energy generated by anger can help us run fast and get an adult to help.

d. If we feel compassion because we see someone who is sick, the energy generated by compassion can help us patiently care for that person.

e. If we are sad because a pet has been hit by a car and has a broken leg, the energy generated by sadness can help us build a fence to protect our pet.

7. Explain that Jesus always used the energy generated by his emotions in ways that honored God, loved others, and solved problems. God the Holy Spirit lives in people who believe in Jesus so they can use the energy generated by their emotions in ways that honor God, love others, and solve problems (John 14:15–16).

8. Thank God that he made us people with feelings.

9. Ask God to help the children use the gift of feelings the way he says to use them.

Options:

Emoticons printed from the Internet may be used to supplement the children's drawings.

Review:

1. Review Lesson 5, and encourage the children to use the energy generated by emotions to trust God through the twists, turns, and tunnels of their lives.

2. When the children are upset, let them choose pictures from the box to show how they are feeling.

3. Encourage the children to believe that God is so mighty he can help the children bring their feelings in line with God's Word.

Notes

4. Ask God to work in them so they use the energy generated by their feelings to honor God, love others, and solve problems.

5. Help the children find ways to use the energy generated by their feelings to know, trust, honor, love, and obey God in difficult circumstances.

NOTES

Lesson 11

Righteous and Unrighteous Anger

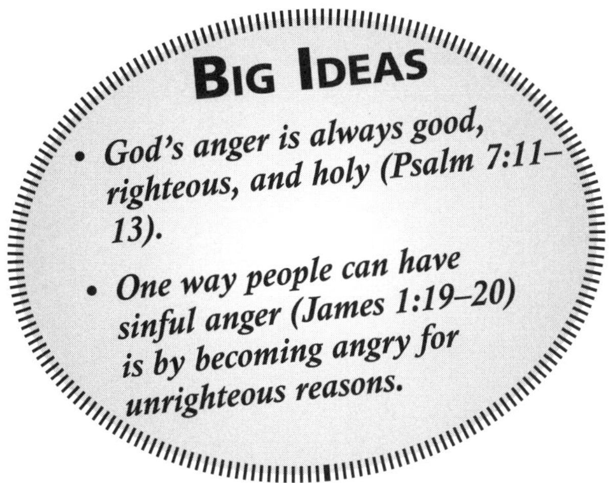

Big Ideas
• God's anger is always good, righteous, and holy (Psalm 7:11–13).
• One way people can have sinful anger (James 1:19–20) is by becoming angry for unrighteous reasons.

Materials

- Bible
- Download Picture-16 *Lightning* (see page 287)
- Poster board mountain (from Lesson 1)
- Disfigured paper mountain (from Lesson 2)
- Paper, scissors, and markers

Activity:

1. Thank God that everything he thinks, says, feels, and does is always good, righteous, and holy. Ask God to make each of you become like him.

2. Pique the children's interest by asking if anger is a gift from God. Explain that anger is an emotion, and emotions are gifts from God that must be used the way he says.

3. Read Genesis 4:1–12. Explain the following:

   a. Cain should have trusted in the Savior God promised to send (Genesis 3:15) and worshiped in a way that honored God's goodness, righteousness, and holiness.

   b. Cain did not honor God's goodness, righteousness, and holiness (1 John 3:12). God had a good, righteous, and holy displeasure toward Cain.

   c. Cain became angry with God, instead of being angry at what angered God (Cain's sin). Instead of putting the energy generated by his anger into honoring God by asking his forgiveness and solving the problem caused by his sin, Cain

Notes

sinfully misused the gift of emotions, hated his brother, and made his problems worse.

4. Explain that situations in which we feel angry can be compared to flashes of lightning. In Genesis 4, the lightning bolt is Cain's unacceptable worship. Place the lightning bolt between the two mountains (representing God's perfect character and people's sin).

5. Use the paper and markers to make a beautiful, pure river. Cut it and place it on the poster board mountain so it flows down the mountain representing God's character. Explain that this is a picture to show that everything God did was good, righteous, and holy. Because God is good, righteous, and holy, he questioned Cain, urged him to follow God's way, and warned him not to crash by following his own way.

6. Read and discuss James 1:19–20. Explain that, as Cain was angry for the wrong reasons, we often sin by being angry at things that do not displease God.

7. Use the paper and markers to make a filthy, polluted river. Cut it and place it on the paper mountain so it flows down the disfigured mountain. Explain that this is a picture to show that Cain's sinful responses flowed from his sin nature. Instead of turning to God, Cain used the energy generated by anger to kill his brother (Genesis 4:8) and lie to God (Genesis 4:9). Like Cain, we often respond to the lightning bolts of our circumstances in sinful ways.

8. Read Psalm 7:11–12. Point back to the river (representing God's perfect thoughts, desires, feelings, and actions) that flows down the mountain (representing God's perfect character). God would not be good, righteous, and holy if he did not punish sin; God's punishment of Cain flowed from his goodness, righteousness, and holiness.

Notes

9. Explain that it is only possible for people to have righteous anger if the flash of lightning they are angry about is something that displeases God: sin. List flashes of lightning that the children become angry about, categorizing them according to whether it is possible to respond to them with righteous anger:

   a. Being told it is time for bed.

   b. Seeing someone hurt another person.

   c. Hearing someone tell lies.

   d. Being told to share with a sibling.

   e. Not getting the first turn with a toy.

   f. Hearing someone mock God.

10. Thank God that Jesus was never angry for the wrong reason. Ask God to help each of you not to sin when lightning flashes around you.

Notes

Options:

Examine other biblical accounts in which people became angry for righteous or unrighteous reasons:

> *1 Samuel 17:26–28.*
> (Eliab was angry because he thought David was boasting; David was concerned about God's honor);
>
> *1 Samuel 20:31–34.*
> (Saul was angry that his son would not be the next king; Jonathan was angry that his father was trying to kill David and thwart God's plan);
>
> *2 Kings 5:11.*
> (Naaman was angry because he thought he deserved more honor from Elisha).

Review:

1. When the children become angry, help them identify the bolt of lightning (the circumstance in which they became angry).

2. Help them discern whether there is any cause for righteous anger.

3. Help them confess unrighteous anger and ask God to deal with any cause for righteous anger.

NOTES

Lesson 12

Forest Fires

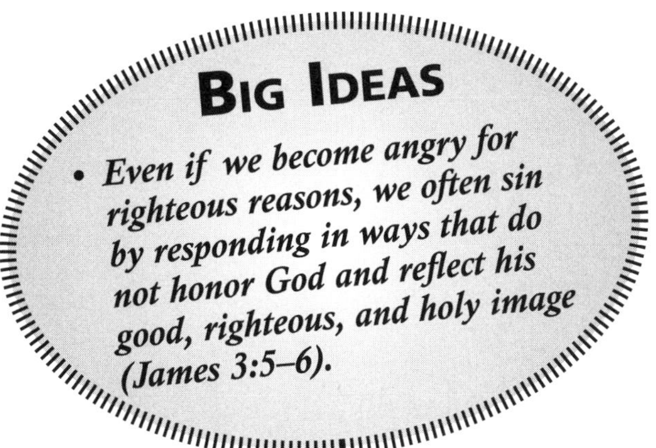

Big Ideas
• Even if we become angry for righteous reasons, we often sin by responding in ways that do not honor God and reflect his good, righteous, and holy image (James 3:5–6).

Materials

- Bible
- Download Picture-16 *Lightning* (see page 287)
- Download Picture-17 *Forest Fire* (see page 287)
- Picture of polluted river (created during Lesson 11)
- Disfigured paper mountain (from Lesson 2)
- Poster board mountain (from Lesson 1)
- Picture of pure river (created during Lesson 11)

Activity:

1. Thank God that Jesus responded to every situation in ways that honored God and reflected his image. Ask God to help each of you respond to every flash of lightning in ways that honor God and reflect his image.

2. Summarize the conflict between Jesus and the Pharisees (the proud religious leaders of Jesus' time), as recorded in Mark. Use the lightning bolt to emphasize how provoking the circumstances were.

   a. When Jesus honored God and reflected his image by forgiving sins, the Pharisees thought he was lying and dishonoring God (2:5–6).

   b. When Jesus honored God and reflected his image by showing mercy to sinners, the Pharisees thought he was dishonoring God (2:16).

   c. The Pharisees acted as if their standards were more important than God's (2:23–28).

3. Read Mark 3:1–5. Identify the flash of lightning in this situation: people were hardhearted, rather than honoring God and reflecting his mercy. Explain this as a situation in which righteous anger is possible.

Notes

4. Discuss ways a person might have responded sinfully to the lightning flash of being accused. Put the polluted river down the disfigured mountain as you discuss these examples.

   a. Some people might have been so sinfully angry about everything that happened in Mark 2 that they wouldn't even have gone to the synagogue to worship God.

   b. Some people might have been thinking so much about the things they were angry about that they wouldn't have noticed the man with the withered hand.

5. Read James 3:5–6. Explain that, often, our sinful response to a flash of lightning is to use words in sinful ways that do not honor God and reflect his image. Place the forest fire on the disfigured mountain to illustrate James 3:5–6 and discuss the following examples:

   a. Starting a yelling match of, "Did not!" and "Did to!" (Proverbs 15:1).

   b. Exaggerating the other person's sin and minimizing our own (Matthew 7:4–5).

   c. Calling the other person names (Matthew 5:22; James 4:11).

   d. Gossiping about someone's sin, rather than talking to the person (Matthew 18:15).

6. Use the poster board mountain (representing God's perfect character) and the pure river (representing the good, righteous, and holy thoughts, words, feelings, and actions that flow from God's righteous character) as you discuss Jesus' good, righteous, and holy responses to the lightning flash of being accused:

   a. Jesus loved the critics by asking a question that could help them better know and love God (Mark 2:8).

   b. Jesus stayed in the synagogue to love both the man with the withered hand and the Pharisees (Mark 3:1–5).

Notes

NOTES

   c. Jesus felt both righteous anger and sorrow over the Pharisees' hardness of heart (Mark 3:5).

7. Thank God that Jesus responded to every flash of lightning in ways that honored God and reflected his image.

8. Ask God to help each of you respond only to the flashes of lightning that reflect God's good, righteous, and holy anger against sin. Ask God to help each of you respond to those flashes of lightning in ways that are good, righteous, and holy.

OPTIONS:

Trace other biblical examples of sinful responses to situations in which it would be possible to have righteous anger. Examples include:

Genesis 27:46.
It would have been possible for Rebekah to have righteous anger that Esau married women who did not follow God's way. Instead of using the energy generated by anger to encourage Jacob to obey God, Rebekah responded sinfully by being disgusted and despairing of life.

Numbers 20:2–12.
It would have been possible for Moses to be angry that the people did not honor God by trusting him. When Moses disobeyed God by striking the rock (20:11), rather than speaking to it as God commanded (20:8), Moses responded sinfully (20:12).

Review:

Notes

1. When the children are angry, help them discern whether it is possible to have righteous anger.

2. When the children respond sinfully, help them trace the polluted river of their responses.

3. Encourage the children to believe that God has power to help them respond to lightning bolts in ways that honor God and reflect his image.[3]

3 Lou Priolo's *The Heart of Anger* is a treasure trove of practical wisdom. Parents and teachers who invest time in helping their children develop and use the Anger Journal and Heart Journal explained in this book will reap a harvest of peaceable fruit.

Lesson 13

Put Out the Fire

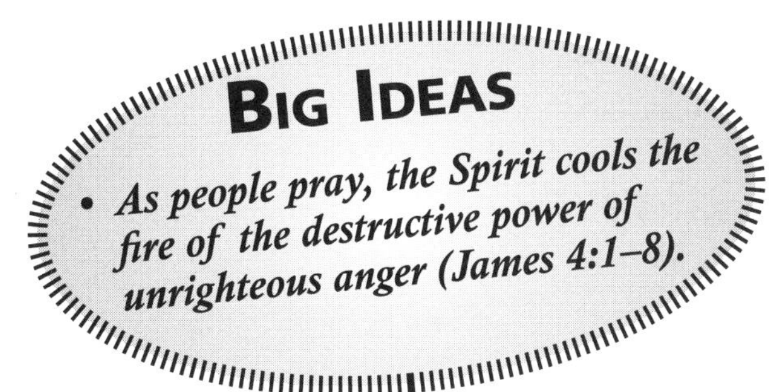

BIG IDEAS
• As people pray, the Spirit cools the fire of the destructive power of unrighteous anger (James 4:1–8).

Materials

- Bible
- Empty two-liter plastic bottle*
- Water*
- Freezer*
- Two metal baking sheets*
- Oven*
- Table
- Pot holders
- Towel
- Electric fan
- Heavy paper
- Pencils or markers

* Advance preparation: partially fill a two-liter plastic bottle with water. Cap the bottle and freeze it until it is solid. Just before the lesson, heat two metal baking sheets to no more than 110°. Set up table near an electrical outlet.

Activity:

1. Thank God that Jesus' perfect life and death on the cross put out the fire of God's wrath for everyone who believes in him.

2. Read James 4:1–8. Explain that, when we respond with sinful anger (James 4:1–3), we oppose God (James 4:4–5). When anger burns hot, we should put the energy generated by anger into praying (James 4:7–8).

3. Explain that Jesus compared God the Holy Spirit to wind (John 3:8). Just as the children cannot see the wind, they cannot see the Holy Spirit. In provoking situations (when lightning strikes), as the children put the energy generated by anger into praying, the Holy Spirit blows like wind to cool the destructive fire of sinful anger.

4. Explain that the following demonstration is a picture of the invisible power of the Holy Spirit working as God's children pray in the midst of provoking situations.

   a. Use pot holders to set the heated baking sheets as far apart as possible on the table (where the children can see, but not touch, them). Make sure the table is not directly against a wall.

b. Wrap a towel around one of the baking sheets. Tell the children this will show what happens when a person holds on to anger.

c. Put the bottle of frozen water behind the baking sheet that is not wrapped in the towel. Tell the children this will show what happens when an angry person prays.

d. Put an electric fan behind the bottle of frozen water and the uncovered baking sheet. Tell the children this fan represents the invisible Holy Spirit who works in us as we pray.

e. Turn on the fan. The baking sheet that represents a person praying about sinful anger and its unrighteous responses will cool very quickly (because the fan and the ice in the bottle work together to cool the surrounding air.)

f. After you test their temperatures, allow children to touch both pans. The children should be able to feel that one pan is still hot, but the other is cool.

g. Draw parallels to the way the Holy Spirit cools the fire of anger as we pray. Thank God for the Holy Spirit's power in cooling the fires of anger.

Notes

Options:

When we are angry, we often sin in the way we speak to and/or about others.

1. Memorize James 3:5 (and following verses, if desired).

2. Ask God to help each of you speak to him about provoking circumstances so your words will not start raging forest fires.

Review:

Notes

1. Begin making a "cue card" to remind the children how to pray in the midst of provoking circumstances.

2. On a piece of heavy paper, have the children draw a lightning bolt. Under the lightning bolt, help them write:

Cue Card #1: Dealing With Anger
1. Ask the Holy Spirit to cool the fire of anger.

(Steps will be added to this card in future lessons.)

3. When the children are angry, use the cue card to help them cry out to the Holy Spirit to cool the fire of anger. Thank God for his promise to give the Holy Spirit when his children pray (Luke 11:11–13).

Lesson 14

Repentance

Big Ideas

- *Our actions flow from our hearts (Luke 6:45; Matthew 15:19).*
- *Repentance is turning from our own way to follow God's way (Acts 3:19; Matthew 3:8).*

Materials

- Bible
- Whiteboard or poster board
- Pencils or markers
- Optional: train set or download Picture-15 *Train Engine* (see page 287), and homemade track (from Lessons 3, 4 and 5)
- Download Picture-16 *Lightning* (see page 287); (from Lessons 11 and 12)
- Download Picture-18 *Jonah* (see page 287)
- Tape
- Cue card (from Lesson 13)

Activity:

1. Ask God to help the children follow God's way instead of following their own way.
2. Draw a large **Y** on the whiteboard or posterboard.[4] Write "God's Way" on the right branch of the **Y**. Write "My Way" on the left branch.
3. Review Lesson 2 by reminding the children that, ever since Adam and Eve sinned, people have followed their own sinful ways. Read Acts 2:38 and explain that God commands people to repent—to turn from following their sinful ways to following God's way.
4. Draw a line from the left branch of the **Y** to its right branch; write "Repentance" on that line. Explain how God led you to repent of your sin and turn to Christ for salvation.
5. Explain that, after this repentance to salvation, Christians still sin, but turn back to God's way by repenting (2 Chronicles 7:14; Joel 2:12–13). Explain that Christians do not lose their salvation when they sin, but lose joy (Psalm 51:12)

4 I first saw a **Y** chart during a seminar taught by Pastor Brad Bigney at an Association of Certified Biblical Counselors conference.

Notes

and suffer the consequences of disobedience (Hebrews 12:5–11). They find joy in repentance (Psalm 32; Acts 3:19–20).

6. Tape the lightning bolt at the point where the left and right branches of the **Y** begin to diverge. Explain that, in every situation, we choose to follow God's way or our own way (Deuteronomy 5:32).

7. Tell the children to notice which path Jonah took as you read or retell Jonah 1–3.

   a. God told Jonah to preach to sinful people in Nineveh (Jonah 1:1–2). Jonah did not want to preach to his enemies. Instead of following God's way, Jonah sailed away from Nineveh (1:3). Tape the picture of Jonah on the left side of the **Y**.

   b. God sent a great storm. The sailors were afraid their ship would be shattered (1:4–5). Jonah told the sailors that, if they threw him into the sea, the storm would be over (1:12). When Jonah followed his own way, it caused many problems.

   c. God sent a great fish to swallow Jonah (1:17). Jonah prayed (2:2, 7)—turning back to God's way. Move Jonah across the "bridge of repentance" to the right side of the Y.

   d. The fish spit Jonah out on land (2:10). God told Jonah to preach to the Ninevites (3:1–2). Jonah obeyed (3:3–4). Move Jonah farther along the right side of the **Y**.

   e. The people of Nineveh were so far along the left side of the **Y** that God was going to destroy them for following their way instead of God's way.

   f. The Ninevites repented of their sin, so God did not destroy them (3:5–10).

   g. Jonah was angry that God had compassion on the Ninevites (4:1–4). Emphasize that this was not a situation in which it was not possible to have righteous anger. Move Jonah to the

NOTES

left side of the **Y**. Jonah needed to repent of unrighteous anger.

8. Read Matthew 12:40 and draw parallels between Jonah and Jesus. Jesus, who is greater than Jonah (Matthew 12:41), came to earth, and obeyed God perfectly. Jonah spent three days and nights in the belly of a huge fish because of his own sin, but—after dying on the cross—Jesus spent three days and nights in the belly of the earth because of our sin. Jesus saves those who repent from the heart (Ezekiel 18:30–31). Jonah was angry that sinners repented and received mercy; Jesus welcomes repentant sinners (Luke 15).

9. Thank God that Jesus was swallowed up by God's wrath on the cross so we could live under God's blessing forever. Ask God to help the children keep on repenting by turning away from sin.

Options:

1. Use the **Y** chart to track other biblical examples of repentance or continuing in sin (such as Jonah 4:1–8, Luke 15:11–32, Matthew 21:28–30, and Job 42:1–6).

2. Children can build a **Y** train track and label the branches "God's Way" and "My Way." They can crash the train that follows the "My Way" track and build a joyful place along the other branch of the track.

Notes

Review:

1. Add to Cue Card #1, which you began making in Lesson 13:

> **Cue Card #1: Dealing With Anger**
>
> *2.* Ask God to show you if it is possible to have righteous anger in the situation.
>
> a. If not, repent of sinful thoughts, words, feelings, and actions.
>
> b. If so, ask God to help you not respond sinfully, but use the energy generated by anger to respond in ways that honor God, love people, and solve problems.

2. When the children are angry, use the cue card to remind them to ask for the Spirit to cool the fire of anger.

3. Help them discern whether righteous anger is a possibility. If not, help the children confess any responses that follow their own way, rather than God's. If so, read Ephesians 4:26, 29–32.

4. Pray that God would help the children not to respond sinfully. If the children have already responded sinfully, encourage them to seek forgiveness from God and others.

Notes

Lesson 15

Gaining Perspective

Big Ideas

- *God knows all things (Isaiah 46:9–10); he always has the right perspective on every situation.*
- *People's knowledge about situations is always limited and often wrong (Psalm 139:6).*
- *Worship helps us gain God's perspective (Psalm 73, especially verses 16–17), so we can respond to circumstances in ways that honor God, love people, and solve problems.*

Materials

- Bible
- Picture-4 *Bear Close-up* on page 263 and Picture-5 *Bear in the Zoo* on page 265
- Cue card (from Lessons 13 and 14)
- Pencils or markers

Notes

Activity:

1. Thank God that he knows all things. Ask God to help each of you trust him in all things.

2. Use Picture-4 *Bear Close-up* on page 263 and Picture-5 *Bear in the Zoo* on page 265 to contrast a limited perspective and a broader perspective. The picture of the bear from the limited perspective could be frightening, but the broader perspective shows the bear is in the zoo. The difference between the limited perspective and the broader perspective of the two pictures is nothing compared to the difference between our limited perspective as fallen creatures and the all-knowing perspective God has on all things.

3. Read Isaiah 46:9–10 and explain that God's knowledge is perfect. Emphasize that God always has a perfect perspective on every situation.

4. Read Psalm 139:6 and explain that, even before Adam and Eve sinned, human knowledge was limited. Now, people's knowledge is both limited and marred by sin. Emphasize that people's knowledge about situations is always limited and often wrong.

5. As you read or retell the story of Esther, help the children see what different perspectives the people and God had on each situation.

    a. Because of their sin, the Israelites had been forced to leave the Promised Land (2 Chronicles 36:14–21). So, Hadassah was growing up in Persia (Esther 2:5–7). Because the Persian king wanted a wife (Esther 1), Hadassah had to hide her identity and go into the king's palace with other young women. This probably looked like a crisis to Hadassah (who was also called Esther), but God had a perfect perspective and plan. The king made Esther his queen (Esther 2:17).

    b. Haman, the king's vice-regent, hated Mordecai because Mordecai would bow only to God, not to Haman (Esther 3:2–5). Haman had unrighteous anger. Haman responded sinfully and used the energy generated by his anger to plan to kill all the Jews (Esther 3:6–15). Mordecai and Esther were grieved by Haman's plan (Esther 4:1–4), but God had a perfect perspective and plan.

    c. Mordecai told Esther to ask the king to save the Jewish people even though Esther could be killed for going to the king without his invitation (Esther 4:11). This looked like a crisis to Esther, but God had a perfect perspective and plan. Mordecai reminded Esther of God's perspective: God would save his people, but if Esther refused to act, God would not save her. Mordecai said that God might have planned to make Esther queen in order to deliver his people (Esther 4:13–15). Esther's perspective was changed as she looked at the situation from God's perspective. She asked her people to fast

Notes

and pray. She was willing to face her death (Esther 4:16).

d. Esther made a wise plan to invite the king and Haman to two banquets before pleading that the king save the lives of her people (Esther 5–7). When the king learned of Haman's plan, Haman and his sons were hanged on the gallows Haman had built for Mordecai (Esther 7:10). The king decreed that the Jewish people could kill their enemies (Esther 8). After defeating their enemies, the Jewish people celebrated their victory (Esther 9:18–32). God's people were delivered because God had a perfect plan that came from his perfect perspective.

6. Explain that, when we face provoking circumstances, we honor God by believing that his perspective and plan are better than ours. As we know God better through worship (by praying, hearing/reading Scripture, listening to sermons, or singing his praises), we gain the perspective of faith and are strengthened to trust God.

7. Thank God that he always has a perfect plan that comes from his perfect knowledge of every situation. Ask God to help you trust him in difficult situations.

Notes

Options:

Have the children act out the story of Esther while you serve as narrator by drawing attention to the difference between Esther's initial perspective and God's omniscient perspective.

Review:

Add the following steps to Cue Card #1:

Cue Card #1: Dealing with Anger

3a. Worship God by praying, reading his Word, or singing his praises. Ask God to help you see this situation from the perspective of faith and trust his perfect plan.

b. Ask God to show you how to respond in ways that honor him, love others, and solve problems.

Lesson 16

Attack The Problem

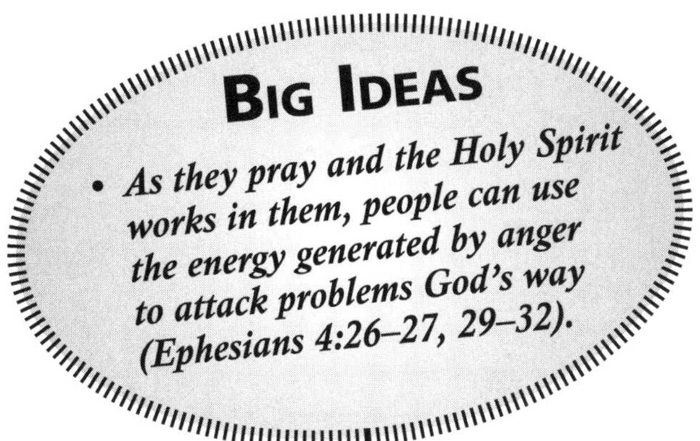

BIG IDEAS
• As they pray and the Holy Spirit works in them, people can use the energy generated by anger to attack problems God's way (Ephesians 4:26–27, 29–32).

Materials

- Bible
- Whiteboard or large paper
- Whiteboard markers
- Optional: paper, pencils and markers
- Picture-6, *Four-Part Drawing* on page 267
- Cue card (from Lessons 13–15)

Notes

Activity:

1. Thank God that, on the cross, Jesus attacked the problem of our sin. Ask God to help each of you use the energy generated by anger to attack problems God's way.

2. Review Lesson 13 by reminding the children that, as they pray, the Holy Spirit cools the fire of anger (James 4:1–8).

3. Read Ephesians 4:26–27 and 29–32. Explain that God's Word shows us how to direct the energy fueled by anger to attack problems and solve them God's way. On the whiteboard or large paper, list things this passage tells us to attack and things this passage tells us not to attack:

   Attack:

   a. Your anger before the sun goes down
   b. Opportunities the Devil offers to sin
   c. Sinful talk
   d. Bitterness, rage, and anger

   Do not attack:

   a. **The Holy Spirit** or
   b. **Other people**, but be kind, tenderhearted, and forgiving to them—as God has been to you.

4. Read and discuss the following verses to show the children how to attack the problem, rather than attacking other people:

Proverbs 15:1	Speak gently.
Proverbs 15:2	Speak wisely.
Proverbs 15:4	Speak truthfully.
Proverbs 15:5, 10	Obey God and other authorities.
Proverbs 15:18	Wait and work patiently.
Proverbs 15:19	Work diligently.
Proverbs 15:22	Seek help from wise people.
Proverbs 15:24, 32	Follow God's way.

5. Read Romans 5:9. Explain that Jesus attacked our worst problem: the sin that put us under God's wrath. Likewise, the problem we often need to attack is our sin.

6. Read Ephesians 4:20–24. Explain that God's Spirit helps us attack our sin by putting it off—like throwing off clothes that have been sprayed by a skunk.

7. Thank God that Jesus attacked our sin instead of attacking us. Ask God to make us like him so we attack problems, not people.

Options:

Have the children make four-part drawings.

In the first box, they should show a situation in which they would be tempted to become angry.

In the second box, they should show the sinful response they would be tempted to make.

Notes

In the third box, they should show themselves praying.

In the fourth box, they should draw themselves doing something that shows how the Holy Spirit changed them as they prayed.

An example of a four-part drawing that coincides with a later lesson (showing a puppet reacting with sinful anger when he was told he could not use playdough but could draw) is given in Picture-6 *Four-Part Drawing* on page 267.

NOTES

REVIEW:

On Cue Card #1, add the following:

CUE CARD #1: DEALING WITH ANGER
4a. Ask God to give you power to attack the problem, not the person.

1. When the children are upset, help them use the cue card. Then make a chart showing what they should and should not attack.

2. Review the verses from Step 4 of this lesson.

3. Ask the children which verse(s) they plan to follow.

4. Help them make and carry out a plan to attack the problem in a way that honors God.

Lesson 17

Don't Blow Up!

Big Ideas

- *The emotion of anger is a gift from God (1 Timothy 6:17; James 1:17) that must be used the way God says to use it (1 Corinthians 10:31).*
- *God wants us to use the energy generated by anger to obey God, love people, and solve problems. We don't solve problems by blowing up (Ephesians 4:29, 31–32); we use the energy generated by anger to solve problems God's way (Ephesians 4:26–27, 29–32).*

Materials

- Bible
- Clay
- Glass dish or metal baking sheet
- Baking soda
- Vinegar
- Optional: paper, pencils and markers
- Picture-6 *Four-Part Drawing* on page 267
- Cue card (from Lessons 13–16)

Notes

Activity:

1. Thank God that Jesus used his energy to solve the terrible problem of our sin. Ask God to help the children use the gift of energy to listen well so they can know God better.

2. Read and discuss Mark 3:1–5 as an example of Jesus' righteous anger.

3. Ask the children if it is easy to sit still and keep quiet when they are angry. Some people have a hard time sitting still and keeping quiet when they are angry because anger is a response that fuels energy. Some people misuse that energy by blowing up. Following their own way, they sin by speaking unkindly, throwing things, hitting, or blowing up in other ways.

4. Read Proverbs 29:11a, "A fool gives full vent to his anger." Explain that blowing up is giving full vent to anger. God says fools blow up.

5. Make a volcano out of clay, leaving a hollow tube-like space in the center of the volcano's peak. Put the volcano in a glass baking dish or metal baking sheet for easy cleanup. Explain that the tube within the volcano is called a vent, and this volcano represents a person who uses the energy generated by anger to blow up. Put baking soda in the vent.

6. Seat the children where they can see the volcano. Pour vinegar into the vent. During the eruption, tell the children this is a picture of the fool who gives full vent to his anger. Tell the children not to touch the volcano after it erupts because the vinegar may sting. Explain that anger also burns; blowing up burns the people around the angry person.

7. Read Proverbs 29:11, emphasizing that wise people control the way they express their emotions.

8. Read and explain Ephesians 4:26, 29, 31–32. God wants us to use the energy fueled by anger to solve problems by speaking words that build others up, forgiving others, and doing kind and compassionate acts for others. When we use the energy generated by anger to blow up, we do not honor God, love people, or solve problems.

9. Thank God that he did not blow up because of our sin (Romans 5:9), but used his energy to save us from our sin. Explain that his Spirit can give his children power to use the energy generated by anger to honor God, love people, and solve problems.

10. Ask God to forgive each of you for sinful misuses of anger. Thank him for his power.

Notes

Options:

Notes

Red food coloring may be added to the vinegar to color the volcanic "lava." Liquid dishwashing soap may be added to the vinegar to create foamy "lava."

Review:

On Cue Card #1 add the following 4b:

> **Cue Card #1: Dealing With Anger**
>
> *4b.* Ask God to give you his power, which is greater than a volcano's power, not to blow up.

1. When the children face provoking circumstances, help them work through the cue card.

2. Help them repent of blowing up by asking God's forgiveness, thinking of ways to solve their problems, then using the energy fueled by their anger to honor God, love others, and solve problems.

Lesson 18

Don't Clam Up!

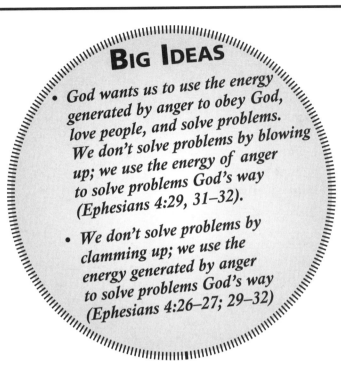

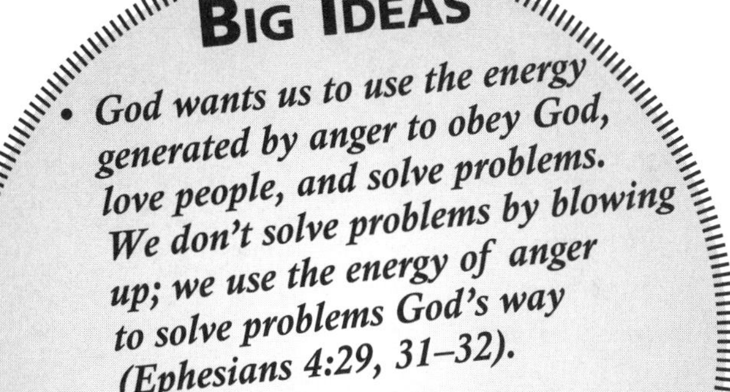

Big Ideas
• God wants us to use the energy generated by anger to obey God, love people, and solve problems. We don't solve problems by blowing up; we use the energy of anger to solve problems God's way (Ephesians 4:29, 31–32).
• We don't solve problems by clamming up; we use the energy generated by anger to solve problems God's way (Ephesians 4:26–27; 29–32)

Materials

- Bible
- Picture-7 *Clams* on page 269
- Picture-8 *Volcano* on page 271
- Paper bag
- Scissors
- Glass dish or metal baking sheet
- Baking soda
- Vinegar
- Cue card (from Lessons 13–17)
- Pencil or markers

Activity:

1. Thank God for Jesus, who saves us from God's righteous anger against sin. Ask God to help the children put God's gift of energy into learning how to solve problems God's way.

2. Ask if some of the children become quiet or even refuse to talk when they are angry. Explain that people sometimes clam up and keep the energy generated by anger inside. They follow their own way instead of honoring God, loving others, and solving problems.

3. Contrast Picture-8 *Volcano* on page 271 and Picture-7 *Clams* with their shells closed on page 269. Contrast responses that spew out anger and those that hold it inside. Have children demonstrate what clamming up looks like. Explain that, when we keep the energy generated by anger

Notes

inside and clam up, we do not honor God, love others, or solve problems.

4. Read Ephesians 4:26–27. Explain that, when we are angry, we should use the energy fueled by anger to solve the problem as soon as possible (before the sun goes down).

5. Cut horizontally across a paper bag, retaining the lower one-third of the bag to be a paper volcano. Put the paper volcano in a glass baking dish or metal baking sheet for easy cleanup. Put baking soda inside the paper volcano. Tell the children this volcano represents someone who keeps anger inside by clamming up.

6. Pour vinegar into the bag. Pour at such a rate that the eruption never goes above the top of the paper bag. After pouring, use your hand to clamp the bag shut.

7. Pick up the volcano. Show the children that it has a hole in the bottom. The volcano has destroyed itself by holding in anger. When we clam up by holding in our anger, the devil gets a foothold in our lives that can destroy us (Ephesians 4:26–27).

8. Explain that Jesus did not clam up in heaven but came to save us from our sin.

9. Ask God to forgive each of you for clamming up. Ask God to help you use the energy generated by anger to obey God, love others, and solve problems.

Options:

Read Hebrews 12:14–15 and discuss the dangers of bitterness.

Notes

Review:

On the cue card you have been making, under Step 4b, add the following:

Cue Card #1: Dealing With Anger
4c. Ask God to give you his power not to clam up.

1. Every time the children refuse to talk about problems, remind them that keeping the energy generated by anger inside does not honor God, love others, or solve problems.

2. Help them talk to God about their hurt and anger, then use God's gift of energy to work out problems in loving ways that honor God.

Notes

Lesson 19

Fear and Trust

Big Ideas

- *Fear is a gift from God that alerts us to dangers God wants to protect us from and problems God wants us to solve; we can face fearful situations by putting our faith in God (1 Samuel 17).*

Materials

- Bible

Notes

Activity:

1. Ask God to help the children use his gift of energy to listen well and know God better.

2. Pique the children's interest by asking if fear is a gift from God. Explain that fear is an emotion; like other emotions, it is a gift that must be used the way God says.

3. When we feel afraid, God does not want us to use the energy generated by fear to "freak out" by screaming, wailing, or worrying. God does not want us to use the energy generated by fear to "hide out"—so frightened that we cannot act to protect ourselves and others in ways that honor God. God wants us to use the energy generated by fear to know and trust him. God wants us to use the energy generated by fear to solve problems in ways that honor God, and protect ourselves and others from the dangers God wants us to avoid.

4. As you read or retell this account from the Bible, have the children demonstrate ways people responded to their feelings of fear. When the children hear of someone who freaked out, they

should look crazed with fear; when they hear of someone who hid out, they should cower in fear.

5. Read 1 Samuel 17:1–11. Discuss the following questions:
   a. How did the Israelite soldiers feel?
   b. Why do you think they freaked out?
6. Read 1 Samuel 17:12–16. Discuss the following questions:
   a. How long did this situation go on?
   b. Why did the Israelite soldiers hide out for forty days instead of using the energy generated by fear to love and protect all the people of Israel?
7. Read 1 Samuel 17:17–26. Discuss the following:
   a. What did the Israelite soldiers do when they saw Goliath?
   b. When we use the energy generated by fear to freak out, we do not honor God, love people, or solve problems.
8. Reread 1 Samuel 17:26, telling the children to listen for what David thought when he heard Goliath. Help the children contrast what the Israelite soldiers thought and did, with what David thought and did. The Israelite soldiers thought about Goliath's size and strength, so they freaked out and hid out. David thought about God's perfect character and how to remove this dishonor from God's people.
9. Read 1 Samuel 17:32. Help the children see that David wanted to fight Goliath to lovingly protect the Israelite soldiers from continuing to lose courage.
10. Read 1 Samuel 17:33–35. Help the children see that David fought the lion and the bear to protect the sheep from danger.

Notes

11. Read 1 Samuel 17:36–37 and emphasize that David did not focus on Goliath's strength but on God's power. In this way, David climbed the mountain of God's perfect character (as discussed in Lesson 15) to get God's perspective on his situation. Explain that trusting God's perfect character helps Christians not to freak out or hide out in frightening circumstances. Trusting a very big God empowers people to respond to frightening situations in ways that honor God.

12. Read 1 Samuel 17:37–47. Emphasize that fear was not the engine that drove David's actions. David's thoughts about God's honor and his faith in God's power drove David's actions. Read 1 Samuel 17:48–51, then end by reading verse 47 again.

13. Hebrews 12:2 tells us to keep "our eyes on Jesus, the champion who initiates and perfects our faith" (New Living Translation). Explain that Jesus is a better champion than David. Our biggest problem is being under the wrath of God. Jesus is a champion, far better than David, who faced God's fearsome wrath on the cross. Jesus faced this dreadful situation by focusing on honoring God and saving his people.

14. Read 1 Peter 2:23 and explain how Jesus' faith in God's character kept him from being controlled by fear when he faced God's wrath on the cross.

15. Ask God to help the children trust Jesus, their warrior, champion, and protector, in scary situations.

Options:

1. Help the children act out the account of David and Goliath.

2. Memorize Psalm 56:3–4 or Isaiah 41:10. Help the children apply these verses as they face frightening situations.

Notes

Review:

1. When the children are afraid, pray that God will help them focus on trusting God's perfect character, especially his love.

2. Help the children repent of using the energy generated by fear to freak out and hide out.

3. Help them think of ways to use the energy generated by fear to protect themselves and others and solve problems in ways that honor God.

Notes

Take Your Fear to God

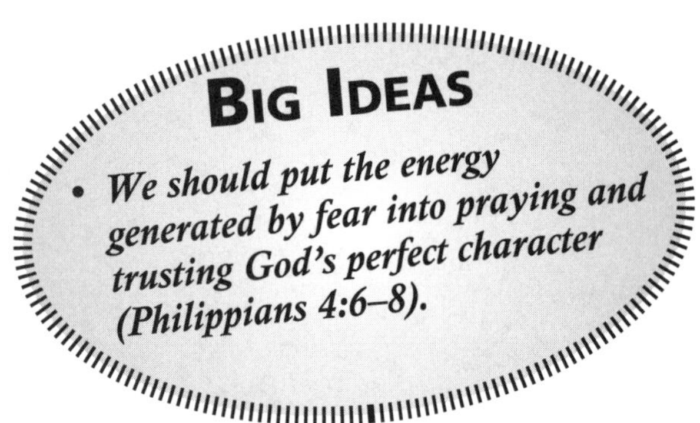

Big Ideas
• We should put the energy generated by fear into praying and trusting God's perfect character (Philippians 4:6–8).

Materials

- Bible
- Heavy paper
- Pencils or markers

Notes

Activity:

1. Thank God that we can talk to him about all our problems and trust his perfect character.

2. As you read or retell the events of Isaiah 36 and 37, have the children listen to find out how people responded to frightening situations (instead of hiding out or freaking out).

   a. Sennacherib, the king of the cruel and powerful Assyrians, had captured the cities of Judah (36:1). He sent a messenger to Jerusalem to mock the puny army of Judah and mock its king for trusting God (36:4–10).

   b. The messenger told the people of Judah not to listen to Hezekiah when he told them to trust God (36:13–15). The messenger promised that the people's lives would go well if they refused to obey their king by trusting God (36:16–17).

   c. The men of Judah who heard this messenger did not freak out or hide out. They did not not speak a word to the messenger but told King Hezekiah about the situation (36:21–22).

   d. Filled with grief, Hezekiah went to the temple to pray (37:1). He asked Isaiah to pray that God would rebuke Sennacherib for mocking God (37:2–4).

Notes

e. Sennacherib's messenger brought Hezekiah a letter reminding him that Sennacherib had destroyed many other lands (37:10–13).

f. Hezekiah took the letter to the temple to show it to God (37:14).

3. Read Isaiah 37:15–20. Ask what Hezekiah did instead of freaking out or hiding out. Emphasize that Hezekiah and his men did not talk to the messenger, but talked to God. Discuss ways Hezekiah climbed the mountain of God's perfect character to gain perspective on his situation. Discuss ways Hezekiah prayed about the reality of his frightening circumstances (37:18) and the reality of God's perfect character (37:16, 20). Discuss Hezekiah's motive (honoring God; 37:17–20).

4. Finish the account of God's work by explaining the following:

   a. God acknowledged that Sennacherib was mocking God's character (37:23–26).

   b. God said he was in control of the situation. God had given Sennacherib victory against other cities (37:26–28).

   c. God said he would punish Sennacherib (37:29).

   d. God promised to save his people by his power (37:30–32).

   e. God said he would defend Jerusalem for the sake of his name and his promise to King David (37:35). Sennacherib would not take Jerusalem, but would return to his own land (37:33–34).

   f. God sent his angel to strike down the Assyrians (37:36). When the Assyrians awoke to find 185,000 of their soldiers dead, they returned home (37:37). There, Sennacherib's sons killed him while he was worshiping idols (37:38).

5. Read Philippians 4:6–8. Write the following steps on Cue Card #2, to help the children remember how to respond to frightening situations in ways

Notes

that protect themselves and others in ways to honor God.

1. Ask God to help you trust him.

2. Ask God to give you his peace (Philippians 4:7).

3. Instead of freaking out or hiding out, tell God about your situation. Ask God to protect you and others (Philippians 4:6). Ask God if there is anything he wants you to do to honor him, love people, or solve problems.

4. Guard your heart and mind by thinking about God's perfect character (Philippians 4:7–8).

6. Thank God that we can come to him in every frightening situation. Ask God to help each of you know his perfect character well enough to trust him in every circumstance.

Cue Card #2: Dealing With Fear

1. Ask God to help you trust him.

2. Ask God to give you his peace (Philippians 4:7).

3. Instead of freaking out or hiding out, tell God about your situation. Ask God to protect you and others (Philippians 4:6). Ask God if there is anything he wants you to do to honor him, love people, or solve problems.

4. Guard your heart and mind by thinking about God's perfect character (Philippians 4:7–8).

Options:

1. The Bible often assures us that, because of God's perfect character, we need not fear.
2. Have the children illustrate any of the following verses:

   Deuteronomy 31:6–8

   Isaiah 41:10

   1 Peter 5:7

   Hebrews 13:5–6
3. Post the illustrated verses where you can see them often. Prayerfully recite them when the children face frightening circumstances.

Notes

Review:

1. Review the account of Esther (from Lesson 15).
2. Ask the children to listen for what Esther does instead of freaking out or hiding out: trust God's perfect character (Esther 4:15–16) and love others (Esther 7:3–4 and 8:3).
3. Explain that Christ, instead of being controlled by fear, trusted God and loved his people by dying on the cross. Because God is holy and righteous, he must punish sin (Nahum 1:3). So, it should be far more fearful for sinners to approach God's throne than it was for Esther to approach the king's throne. Because Christ died for his people, however, those who believe in him are welcomed at God's throne (Hebrews 4:14–16).
4. Use the cue card often to remind the children to trust God's perfect character instead of being controlled by fear.

Lesson 21

Take Your Sadness to God

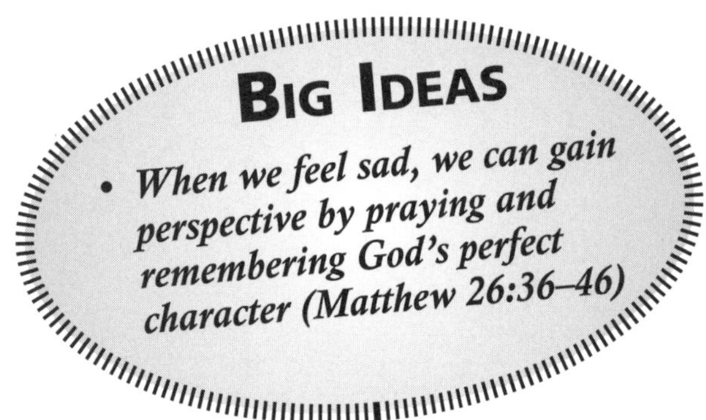

Big Ideas
• When we feel sad, we can gain perspective by praying and remembering God's perfect character (Matthew 26:36–46)

Materials

- Bible
- Train set or download Picture-15 *Train Engine* (see page 287), and homemade track (from Lessons 3, 4 and 14)
- Toy caboose or download Picture-19 *Caboose* (see page 287)
- Adhesive labels or paper, marker, tape, scissors

Notes

Activity:

1. Thank God that Jesus understands, and helps us with, our sadness.

2. Read 1 Samuel 1:1–7. Help the children understand why Hannah was so sad that she would not eat.

3. Read 1 Samuel 1:9–11. Emphasize that Hannah talked to God about her sadness.

4. Read 1 Samuel 1:18b–20. Emphasize that, when Hannah worshiped God, she gained his perspective. God helped her bring her feelings in line with God's Word.

5. Read Matthew 26:26–36. Have the children point out words and phrases that highlight Jesus' deep sorrow. Explain that, as they prayed, both Hannah and Jesus gained God's perspective and trusted God's perfect character.

6. Contrast God's response to the prayers of Hannah and Jesus. God answered Hannah's prayer by giving her the son she asked for. God did not answer Jesus' prayer by sparing him from God's wrath on the cross. Emphasize that, whether or not God grants our requests, the Holy Spirit works

in us as we pray so we can gain God's perspective and trust God's perfect character.

7. Use 1 Samuel 2 to explain what Christ did on the cross in taking our sin and suffering the judgment we deserve under the wrath of God:
   a. Feeble Hannah was strengthened (1 Samuel 2:4), but Christ was broken as he died under the arrows of God's wrath (Isaiah 53:4–5).
   b. Hannah was satisfied (1 Samuel 2:5), but Christ thirsted (John 19:28).
   c. Hannah would no longer be barren and forlorn (1 Samuel 2:6, 21), but Christ was forlorn and forsaken (Matthew 27:37–46; Isaiah 53:8).
   d. God brought life to Hannah (1 Samuel 2:6), but death to Christ (Isaiah 53:10).
   e. God exalted Hannah and enriched her life (1 Samuel 2:7), but abased Christ and made him poor (2 Corinthians 5:21 and 8:9).
   f. God raised Hannah from the dust and ashes (1 Samuel 2:8), but laid Christ in the dust of death (Psalm 22:15).
   g. God gave Hannah a seat of honor (1 Samuel 2:8), but put Christ to shame (Luke 18:32).
   h. God guarded Hannah's feet (1 Samuel 2:9), but crushed Christ (Isaiah 53:10).
8. Thank God that Christ understands our sorrows. Thank God that Jesus died so that we could have joy in God forever. Ask God to help the children talk to him about their sadness and trust God's perfect character in times of sorrow.

Options:

Contrast Hannah's response to her sorrowful situation with Rachel's response to a similar situation (in Genesis 30:1). Especially note that Hannah dealt with

Notes

her strong feelings by talking to God, while Rachel was controlled by her feelings and talked in a demanding way to her husband.

Notes

Review:

1. Write "God and His Word" on the adhesive label or paper.

2. Put it on Picture-15 *Train Engine* on page 287 (first used in Lesson 3).

3. Write "Feelings" on the adhesive label or paper.

4. Put it on the toy caboose or Picture-19 *Caboose* (see page 287). Run this train around the toy or homemade track, reminding the children that, although feelings are important to God, their feelings are not the engine that drives their lives.

5. When the children are upset (whether they are sad, afraid, or angry), use the train track to remind them that God and his Word rule their feelings.

6. Help the children pray that God would bring their feelings in line with his Word.

Lesson 22

Stomp Out Sin

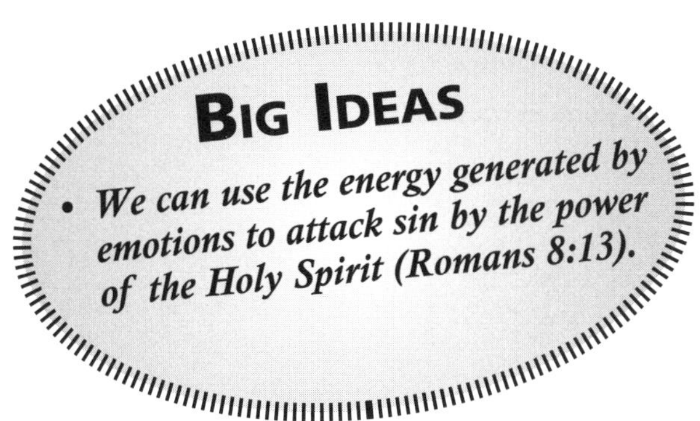

Big Ideas
• We can use the energy generated by emotions to attack sin by the power of the Holy Spirit (Romans 8:13).

Materials

- Bible
- Whiteboard or large paper; markers
- Both cue cards (from Lessons 13–18 and Lesson 20)

Activity:

1. Thank God for the Holy Spirit and his power.
2. Make three columns on the board or large piece of paper, leaving room to add a fourth column later.

Situation	Feelings	Sinful Response to Anger What I said or did	

3. In the first and second columns, list situations in which the children are tempted to sin and emotions they typically feel in those circumstances. Discuss sinful things the children might do in each situation and record those things in the third column of the chart. Examples shown here:

Situation	Feelings	Sinful Response to Anger What I said or did	
Told to stop watching a DVD and pick up toys	Anger, Sadness	Yell at Mom	
Told to share a favorite toy	Anger	Hit my brother instead of sharing with him	
Someone else got picked to do something special	Jealousy	Make faces at my friend who got to do something special	

4. Read Romans 8:13, emphasizing this phrase: "…by the Spirit you put to death the misdeeds of the body."[5]

5 Explain that the things listed in the third column of the chart are the misdeeds of the body. The Holy Spirit helps us put those sins to death.

5. Read John 14:15–17 and explain that the Holy Spirit gives us power to obey God. Add the fourth column. Brainstorm things the Holy Spirit can give the children power to do in each situation.

Situation	**Feelings**	**Sinful Response to Anger** What I said or did	**Attack the Problem** by stomping out sin
Told to share a favorite toy	Anger	Hit my brother instead of sharing with him	Stomp out selfishness; make a plan for sharing the toy peacefully
Someone else got picked to do something special	Jealousy	Make faces at my friend who got to do something special	Stomp out jealousy; put energy into loving and trusting God

6. Have the children stand, spread apart so they cannot touch each other. Review the chart by going through each situation from the first through the fourth columns. For example, say, "You have to share your favorite toy. You feel the energy generated by anger building up. You are tempted to attack the person you're supposed to share with." Ask the children how they are going to use the energy generated by anger. Let the children shout, "Attack the problem, not the person," while stomping, as if stomping out sin. Remind them that the power to stomp out sin comes from the Spirit. Choose particular children to shout out what they can do to attack the problem.

7. Ask God to help the children stomp out sin by the power of the Holy Spirit.

Options:

When the children are tempted to sin, help them give sin the one-two punch. Teach them that Philippians 2:13 says God gives us the will to obey him (one punch) and the power to obey him by doing new actions (second punch).

Notes

Review:

Notes

1. On both cue cards you have been making (the reminders for how to deal with anger and reminders for how to deal with fear) add the final step:

> **Cue Cards #1 and #2**
>
> *5.* Ask God to give you his power to stomp out sin. Believe the Spirit will give you that power. By faith, stomp out sin.

2. When the children sin, help them fill out a chart explaining the situation, their feelings, the misdeeds of the body, and how they can attack the problem (rather than the person) with the power of the Holy Spirit. This will encourage children to build a habit of resolving problems peacefully.

3. When the children face difficulties, remind them that God is the engineer who designs the course of their lives. He is also the engine who can give them power to know, trust, honor, love, and obey him through all the twists, turns, and tunnels of their lives.

LESSON 23

God's Actions and His Heart

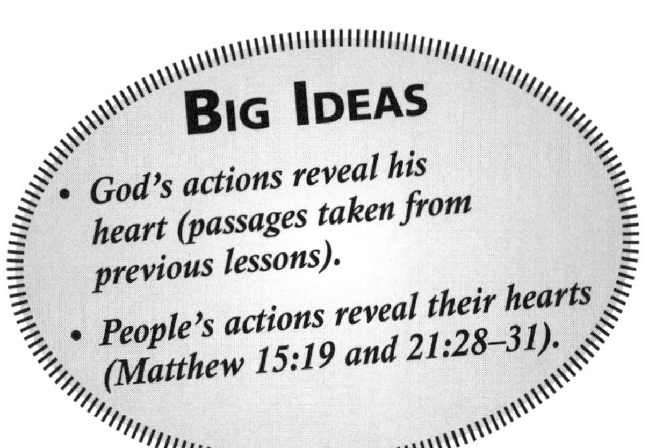

BIG IDEAS
• God's actions reveal his heart (passages taken from previous lessons).
• People's actions reveal their hearts (Matthew 15:19 and 21:28–31).

MATERIALS

- Bible
- Optional: children's picture books

NOTES

ACTIVITY:

1. Ask God to reveal himself to each of you through what he has done.

2. Explain the heart as the part inside each person that feels, thinks, desires, and treasures.

3. Review some of the actions of God as studied in previous lessons, asking questions to help the children see what these actions reveal about God's heart:

   a. Creation (Lesson 1): God's actions in making the world beautiful, providing delicious food, and placing one tree with fruit that Adam and Eve were not to eat reveal the goodness, righteousness, and holiness of his heart.

   b. The Fall (Lesson 2): God's actions of killing an animal to cover people, promising a Savior, and guarding the garden reveal the goodness, righteousness, and holiness of his heart.

   c. The Flood (Lesson 7): God's actions in judging sinners, delivering Noah's family, and promising never again to curse the earth (Genesis 8:21) reveal the goodness, righteousness, and holiness of his heart.

d. Saving his people from famine (Lesson 9): God's actions in preserving Joseph and using Joseph to preserve his people reveal the goodness, righteousness, and holiness of his heart.

e. God's deliverance of Jonah and the people of Nineveh (Lesson 14): God's actions in bringing Jonah to repentance in the belly of the fish and bringing the people of Nineveh to repentance reveal the goodness, righteousness, and holiness of his heart.

f. God's deliverance of Esther and the Israelites (Lesson 15): God's actions in saving Esther's life and using her to save the lives of the Jewish people reveal the goodness, righteousness, and holiness of his heart.

g. God's deliverance of David and the Israelites (Lesson 19): God's actions in honoring his name by saving David's life and using him to save the Israelites reveal the goodness, righteousness, and holiness of his heart.

h. God's deliverance of Hezekiah and the Israelites (Lesson 20): God's actions in honoring his name by saving Hezekiah and using him to save the Israelites reveal the goodness, righteousness, and holiness of his heart.

i. God's delivering Christ to death (Lesson 21): God's actions in delivering his own Son to die in the place of sinners reveal the goodness, righteousness, and holiness of his heart.

4. Read Matthew 21:28–31 and discuss what each son's actions revealed about his heart.

5. Help the children evaluate what some of their recent actions reveal about their hearts. Confess sin and thank God for evidences of his grace.

NOTES

Options:

Notes

Whether you are reading the Bible or children's picture books, watch for and discuss ways people's actions reveal their hearts.

Review:

When the children sin, ask questions to help them see what their actions reveal about their hearts.[6]

6 Tedd Tripp's *Shepherding a Child's Heart*, a book I reread annually while raising children, provides helpful instruction and insight on how to reach a child's conscience by addressing issues of the heart.

Lesson 24

God's Words and His Heart

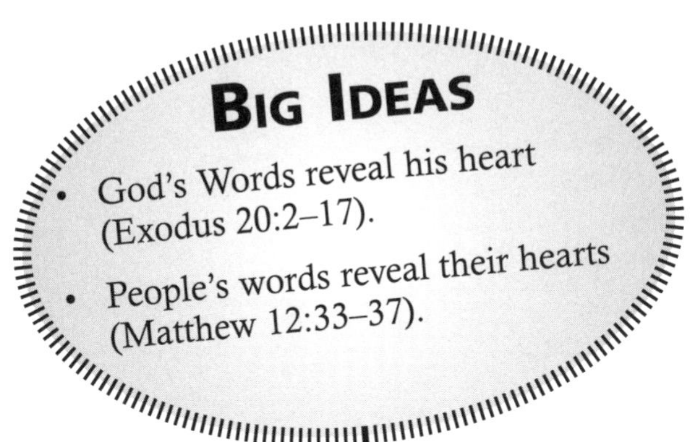

Big Ideas
• God's Words reveal his heart (Exodus 20:2–17).
• People's words reveal their hearts (Matthew 12:33–37).

Materials

- Bible

Notes

Activity:

1. Thank God for revealing himself in his Word. Ask God to help the children see God's heart as they listen to God's Word.

2. Review the definition of the heart as the part of each person that feels, thinks, desires, treasures.

3. Use the following questions to help the children see that God's Ten Words (Decalogue) reveal what God feels, thinks, desires, and treasures. Emphasize the connection between God's Word and his heart.

   a. What does Exodus 20:2 reveal about what God feels, thinks, desires, and treasures? [God showed his glory (Isaiah 63:12–14) by delivering his people (Exodus 6:6–8).]

   b. What do the first and second commandments (Exodus 20:3–6) reveal about what God feels, thinks, desires, and treasures? [God is jealous to be first in our lives; nothing else belongs in first place. God's anger is against those who put anything else in first place (Joshua 23:16; Jeremiah 17:5).]

   c. What does the third commandment (Exodus 20:7) show us about what God feels, thinks, desires, and treasures? [God reveres his name and character and desires that the people he created revere his name, too. God treasures those who honor his name (Malachi 3:16–17).]

NOTES

d. What does the fourth commandment (Exodus 20:8–11) show us about what God feels, thinks, desires, and treasures? [God desires people to be holy (Ezekiel 20:12), to honor him by not working on the Sabbath (Exodus 31:14), and to trust him as provider (Amos 8:5). God desires people to rest in him and delight in him and his creation, as God himself did after creating the world (Genesis 2:2–3). God is displeased with those who dishonor the Sabbath (Jeremiah 17:27).]

e. What does the fifth commandment (Exodus 20:12) show us about what God thinks, feels, desires, and treasures? [God desires all people to be under his authority, and he wants children to learn how to live under his authority by obeying their parents (Ephesians 6:1–3). God is displeased when children disobey their parents (Romans 1:18, 30).]

f. What does the sixth commandment (Exodus 20:13) show us about what God feels, thinks, desires, and treasures? [God values the people he has created in his image and tells us that hating people created in his image is like murder (1 John 3:15).]

g. What does the seventh commandment (Exodus 20:14) show us about what God thinks, feels, desires, and treasures? [God loves covenant loyalty and hates covenant-breaking (Malachi 2:13–16).]

h. What does the eighth commandment (Exodus 20:15) show us about what God thinks, feels, desires, and treasures? [God values honest labor (Exodus 20:9), which he uses to provide for our own needs and those of others (Ephesians 4:28).]

i. What does the ninth commandment (Exodus 20:16) show us about what God feels, thinks, desires, and treasures? [God is truth (John 14:6). God rejoices with the truth

(1 Corinthians 13:6). God hates falsehood (Proverbs 6:16–17).]

j. What does the tenth commandment (Exodus 20:17) show us about what God feels, thinks, desires, and treasures? [God provides for us (Acts 17:24–25) and wants us to trust him enough to be content (Hebrews 13:6).]

4. Read and discuss Matthew 12:33–37. Make sure the children understand that people's words reveal their hearts. Emphasize the fact that no one makes them argue, for example, and no situation makes them complain. Arguing and complaining words come from hearts that are filled with pride and selfishness. Honoring and grateful words come from hearts that are filled with honor and gratitude.

5. Thank God that his good Word reveals the goodness of his heart. Ask God to make each of you become more like God in what you feel, think, desire, and treasure so you can bring forth good words.

Options:

Let the children design an imaginary kingdom where the heart of the king is reflected in the laws of the land. If the king is evil, the children should develop evil laws. If the king is silly, the children should develop silly laws. Use this activity to help the children appreciate God's goodness as revealed in his Ten Words.

Review:

1. When the children sin, help them see how their words and actions reveal their hearts.

2. Help them see how they have violated God's Word that reveals his good, righteous, and holy heart.

3. Lead them in seeking forgiveness and repenting.

Notes

Lesson 25

Dig for Treasure

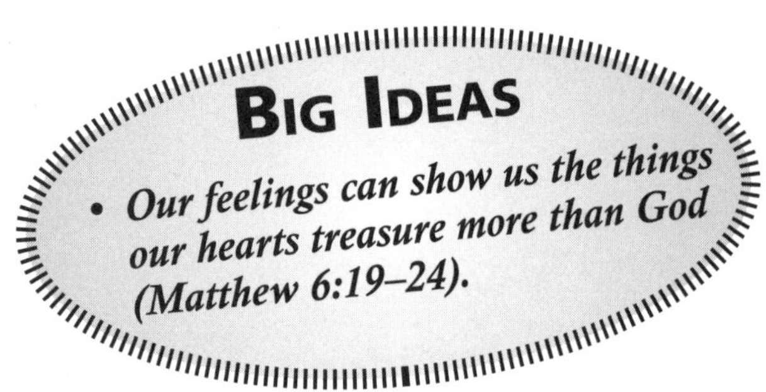

Big Ideas
• Our feelings can show us the things our hearts treasure more than God (Matthew 6:19–24).

Materials

- Bible
- Whiteboard or large paper and markers

Activity:

Notes

1. Ask God to help the children see what they treasure.

2. Read James 4:1–2a. Explain that not using our emotions the way God says causes disagreements.

3. Read Matthew 6:19–21 and 24. Explain that treasuring things more than we treasure God is sin. Explain that the heart is the part of each person that feels, thinks, desires, and treasures. It is the control center that determines people's actions.

4. Tell the children they are going on a treasure hunt to see what kinds of things their hearts treasure. Make a chart[7] that includes the following headings:

Situations	Feelings	Thoughts	Desires	Treasure	Actions

7 This chart is adapted from *Instruments in the Redeemer's Hands*, by Paul David Tripp (Chapter 10).

5. Fill in the chart by starting with situations, feelings, and actions. An example follows:

The Heart—Leads to Actions					
Situations	Feelings	Thoughts	Desires	Treasure	Actions
Told to share a favorite toy	Anger				Grabbing the toy; hiding it so I won't have to share it
Someone else gets picked to do something special	Jealousy				Pouting because I feel sorry for myself

6. Explain that we can't see our body's brains and hearts, but MRIs make pictures of them to help us see if there is anything wrong. We can't see our thoughts, desires, and treasures, but our feelings, like MRIs, can show us what is wrong with what we think, desire, and treasure. Discuss ways of filling in the chart with the thoughts, desires, and treasures that motivate our actions. Examples follow:

Situations	Feelings	Thoughts	Desires	Treasure	Actions
Told to share a favorite toy	Anger	I should be able to play with this toy	Get what I want when I want it	Treasure myself and toys more than God	Grabbing the toy; hiding it so I won't have to share it
Someone else gets picked to do something special	Jealousy	I should get to do special things	Be treated like an important person	Treasure myself more than God and others	Complaining

7. Reread Matthew 6:19–21. Make a new chart to show that treasuring God shapes the heart and the actions that flow from it. After writing the situation, fill in the column labeled Treasure. Then complete the other columns. Finally, add the new action that comes from treasuring God.

Situations	Feelings	Thoughts	Desires	Treasure	Actions
Told to share a favorite toy	Joy in God (even if feeling sad about not playing with the toy)	God is far bigger and better than this toy	Love and enjoy God	Treasuring God more than toys	Asking God to forgive me for loving toys too much; asking God to help me share
Someone else is picked to do something special	Joy	Wow! God loves me!	Rejoice in God's delight in me	Treasuring God	Giving thanks to God; doing something to love the person who was picked

8. Thank God that Jesus always treasured God. Ask God to help each of you treasure him more than anything else.

Options:

The Psalms teach us how to use the energy generated by emotions to treasure God. Read, pray, and sing the psalms often with your children to quiet their hearts and teach them how "faith meets concrete situations."[8]

Review:

1. Every time the children sin, help them do an MRI by examining what their feelings show about their thoughts, desires, and treasures.

2. Help them see how treasuring something more than God keeps them from using the gift of emotions the way God says to use them.

8 *English Standard Version Study Bible*, page 939.

Lesson 26

The Big Squeeze

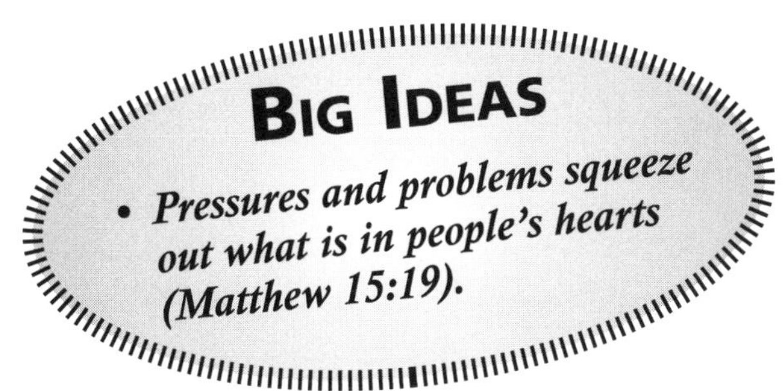

Big Ideas
• Pressures and problems squeeze out what is in people's hearts (Matthew 15:19).

Materials

- Bible
- Quince(s) or lemon(s): enough to produce juice for each child to taste
- Bowl
- Small cup: one per child
- Paper towels
- Bowls: one per child
- Juice oranges: enough for each child to have half

Activity:

1. Ask God to show the children the sweet delight of following God.

2. Ask the children to list some of the pressures of their lives, such as having to sit still, keep quiet, share toys, get along with siblings, etc.

3. Show the children a quince (or lemon). Ask the children to imagine the fruit represents what the Bible calls the heart—the part of them that feels, thinks, desires, and treasures.[9]

4. As you squeeze juice from the fruit into the bowl, tell the children to pretend that every squeeze is one of the pressures they listed. Review the pressures as you squeeze the juice into the bowl.

5. Pour some juice into each child's cup so they can taste its sourness. Emphasize that squeezing the fruit did not cause it to be sour. Squeezing only brought out what was in it.

6. Read and discuss Matthew 15:19a. The quince (or lemon) represents the heart without Jesus. The pressures squeeze out the sourness of sin. Help the children see that the pressures of their lives do not cause them to be angry (or worried, jealous, etc.).

Notes

9 I am indebted to Randy Patten for this idea.

The pressures only bring out what is within them. If the children are filled with themselves and their sin, the pressures will squeeze out the bitter juice of sinful anger (blowing up or clamming up), sinful fear (hiding out or freaking out), etc.

7. Read and discuss Galatians 5:22–23a. Explain that people who believe in Jesus have God's Spirit in their hearts.
8. Give the children paper towels to spread in front of them. Give each child a bowl and half of a juice orange. Explain that the orange represents the heart filled with the Holy Spirit.
9. Have the children squeeze their oranges so the juice drops into the bowl. As the children squeeze the oranges, review the list of pressures. Help the children see that the pressure they are putting on the oranges does not make the juice sweet. The pressure only brings out the juice that is in the orange. Pressures can bring out the sweet fruit of the Spirit in people who are filled with the Holy Spirit. As the children enjoy the orange juice, explain again that, when pressures squeeze the person who is filled with Jesus, the sweetness of Jesus can come out of that person.
10. Thank God for the sweetness of his Holy Spirit. Ask to grow the fruit of the Spirit in each of you.

Options:

Challenge the children not to shift blame to other people or to circumstances for one week.[10] Engage in this activity with them, repenting when you shift blame; acknowledge that the circumstances squeezed out sin that was in your heart.

Notes

10 I am indebted to Rose Marie Miller, who primes the heart for the gospel by giving this assignment to people she disciples: "For one week, do not gossip, complain, blameshift, boast, criticize, or defend yourself." After a week full of silence or repentance, people who do this assignment gain a glimpse of their sinful hearts.

Review:

Notes

1. When the children are frustrated, let them squeeze oranges and drink the juice.
2. Ask God to help the children love him more than anything else, so their pressures will squeeze out "Jesus juice" instead of "sour sin."

Lesson 27

In Hot Water

Big Ideas

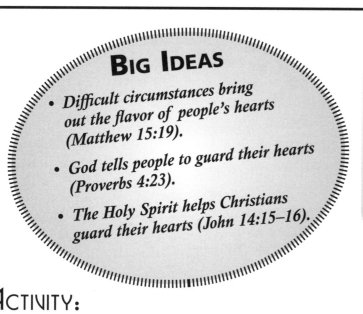

- *Difficult circumstances bring out the flavor of people's hearts (Matthew 15:19).*
- *God tells people to guard their hearts (Proverbs 4:23).*
- *The Holy Spirit helps Christians guard their hearts (John 14:15–16).*

Materials

- Bible
- Small cups: several per child
- Warm water
- Herbal teas of various flavors
- Optional: box and things to slip inside the box

Notes

Activity:

1. Ask God to help the children trust his perfect character in all the difficult circumstances of their lives.

2. Give the children a taste of warm water to see that it is flavorless.

3. Have a tea party,[11] allowing the children to choose and taste various flavors of tea. Discuss ways the warm water brings out the flavor (the sweetness of peppermint tea and the bitterness of dandelion root or cerassee tea, for example).

4. Compare the warm water to difficult circumstances. Difficult circumstances do not cause us to sin; they simply show us the flavor of our hearts.

5. Read Proverbs 4:23. Explain that God commands us to guard our hearts against the bitterness of sin.

6. Discuss what it means to guard something of value:

   a. In art museums, guards protect the paintings so no one can touch them.

11 I am indebted to Randy Patten for this idea.

Notes

b. Guards drive armored cars to keep people from stealing money.

c. People guard their homes by locking doors, using deadbolts, or barring windows.

d. Soccer players wear shin guards to protect their legs from injury.

7. Reread Proverbs 4:23. Explain that, as the "life" of a river flows from its source high in the mountains, our lives flow from our hearts. God commands us to put a priority on guarding our hearts because they are much more important than art, money, homes, or bodies.

8. Discuss things we should guard our hearts against in order to protect the wellspring of our lives: hating others, treasuring things more than God, being jealous of what someone else has, worrying (instead of trusting God), thinking about how other people have hurt us (rather than forgiving them), and being proud about what God has enabled us to be, have, or do, for example.

9. Read John 14:15–17a. Explain that, when people believe in Jesus, God the Father gives them the Holy Spirit to help them obey God's commands. The Holy Spirit helps Christians guard their hearts.

10. Pray, asking the Holy Spirit to help the children guard their hearts.

Options:

Give each child a box to guard all day long. Try to slip something inside the box if the child is not vigilantly guarding it. Remind the children that it is more important and more difficult to guard their hearts from sin than it is to guard a box for one day.

Review:

When the children are upset, invite them to have a cup of tea with you. Over tea, encourage them to pour out their problems to God in prayer. Encourage them to taste the goodness of God (Psalm 34:8) as they sip their tea and trust God's perfect character.

Lesson 28

The Umpire of Your Heart

Big Ideas

- *The peace of Jesus can rule our hearts (Colossians 3:15).*
- *Without self-control, we easily lose peace and are vulnerable to attack (Proverbs 25:28).*

Materials

- Bible
- Blocks

Notes

Activity:

1. Ask God to help the children trust his perfect character, especially his love. Ask God to rule the children's hearts so they can know his peace and joy.

2. Have the children give examples of, and/or model, the differences between people who show self-control and people who do not show self-control.

3. Read Colossians 3:15 and teach the following points:

   a. An umpire enforces rules, keeps order, and rules people out/safe. The word translated as "rule" in Colossians 3:15 was used for the person who made decisions in the ancient Olympic games by enforcing rules, keeping order, and awarding prizes.[12]

   b. Christ's peace is the umpire of our hearts. When we are tempted to be controlled by fear, Christ rules that fear of people and situations, "Out." He gives us his peace to love God, love others, and solve problems. When we are tempted to be controlled by anger, Christ rules our blowing up or clamming up, "Out." He

12 *Gill's Exposition of the Entire Bible*, accessed through Biblehub.com: http://biblecommenter.com/colossians/3–15.htm

gives us his peace to obey God, love others, and solve problems. Christ's peace rules our sinful misuses of emotions "Out," and rules his love, joy, and peace "In."

4. Give examples of learning self-control as the peace of Christ rules the heart:

   a. A child who is afraid of bees can believe that God has given her a spirit of power and love and self-control. She can ask Christ to rule her heart. She can believe that Christ rules her being controlled by fear of bees "Out." She can put her energy into trusting God and loving her friends as she plays outside with them.

   b. A child who is hungry but has to wait for lunch can let Jesus' peace rule him as he waits for lunch without complaining.

   c. Children who do not feel like doing math can let Jesus' peace rule them. They can believe that Jesus will give them power to do their best work. Then they can work cheerfully.

5. Read Proverbs 25:28. Have the children use blocks to build a model of an ancient city and surround it with broken-down walls. Show how easily this city could be attacked. Show how easily the city could lose its peace.

6. Explain that people who do not have Christ's peace ruling their hearts are like this city and cannot have lasting peace. In order to represent the vulnerability of our hearts when we do not submit to Christ as umpire of our emotions, let the children wreck the city. Leave the wreckage standing for the next lesson.

7. Thank God that Jesus is the umpire who rules our hearts. Ask God to give the children a spirit of power and love and self-control.

Notes

Options:

Notes

Walled cities could be violated through small breaches. As the Spirit grows the fruit of self-control in the children, help them notice, and repent of, the smaller breaches of self-control that precede the crashing walls.

Review:

1. When the children are upset, talk and pray with them while they quietly build or draw a walled city.

2. Help them see how not exercising the self-control of the Holy Spirit led to breaking down the protective wall that guards their hearts.

Lesson 29

The Greatest Treasure

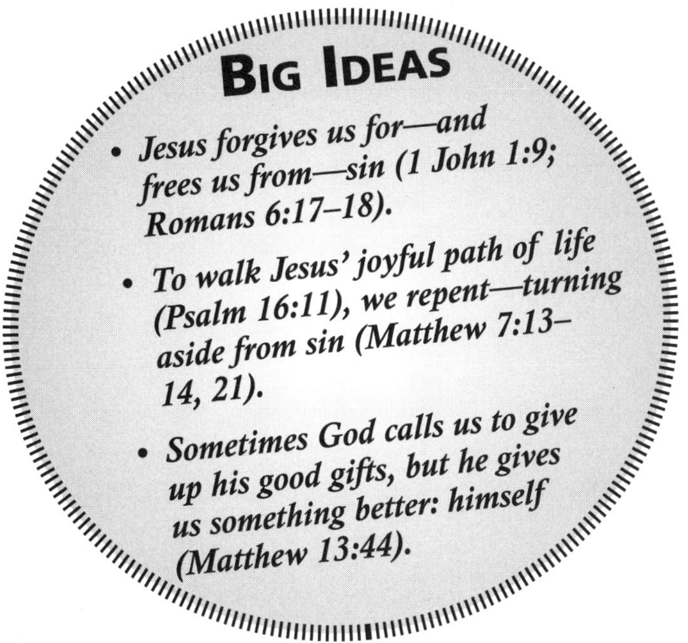

BIG IDEAS
• Jesus forgives us for—and frees us from—sin (1 John 1:9; Romans 6:17–18).
• To walk Jesus' joyful path of life (Psalm 16:11), we repent—turning aside from sin (Matthew 7:13–14, 21).
• Sometimes God calls us to give up his good gifts, but he gives us something better: himself (Matthew 13:44).

Activity:

1. Ask God to make the peace and joy of Jesus rule the children's hearts.

2. Read Psalm 16:11 and point out the path you marked. Explain that you created this path to be a picture of the path of life mentioned in Psalm 16:11.

3. Explain that God gives many good gifts to all people (Matthew 5:45), so both the broken-down city and the path of life contain some of God's good gifts, but only the path of life leads to eternal joy and pleasure (Psalm 16:11).

4. Have the children stand so they can see the ruined city and the path of life. Contrast the narrow gate on the path of life (that must be squeezed through to enter the celebration space) with the wide-open entrance to the broken-down city.

5. Read and discuss Matthew 7:13–14. Ask the children which path they want to follow: the wide

Materials

- Bible
- Place for a celebration*
- Cardboard box and scissors*
- Tape, string, or chalk*
- Food, decorations, and activities for the celebration*
- Rocks (at least one per child) labeled with specific sins: blowing up, clamming up, being controlled by fear, etc.*
- Broken-down city from previous lesson
- Whiteboard and marker or large cross made of paper and taped to a wall*
- Items representing God's good gifts*

* Advance preparation: Prepare a place for a celebration. This place should be behind a very small entrance (cut into a cardboard box). The entrance should be small (just big enough for the children to squeeze through) and closed (so the children cannot see the celebration space inside until the end of the lesson). Mark the route to that celebration place with tape, string, or chalk. Gather materials for activities to be done in that celebration spot. Gather rocks and label them with specific sins. Put the rocks between the broken-down city and the path of life. Display the cross. Gather items that can represent God's good gifts and strew them around the broken-down city and the path you marked.

path of following their own way that leads to being like the ruined city without peace, or the path of life with its fullness of joy.

6. Discuss the sins written on the rocks. Explain that these rocks do not belong on the path of life. Have the children pile the sin-engraved rocks before the cross, as you talk about how Jesus forgives and frees them from those sins (1 John 1:9; Romans 6:17–18).

7. Have the children follow the path of life while gathering the items (representing God's good gifts) that lie along the path.

8. As the children approach the place that has been prepared for the celebration, read Matthew 13:44. Explain that God sometimes calls us to give up his good gifts. Examples follow:

   a. When we are sick, God calls us to give up the good gift of health for a time. We do not know how long that time will be, but he gives us self-control to trust him instead of worrying about how long we will be sick.

   b. When it is time to go to bed, God calls us to cheerfully give up the gift of playing.

   c. When friends move far away, God calls us to give up enjoying their friendship on a regular basis.

   d. Add examples relevant to the losses in the children's lives.

9. Reread Matthew 13:44. Ask the children to give up the items representing some of God's good gifts in order to enter the small opening and gain the joyful surprise prepared for them on the path of life. (After the children enter, remove the box so you can enter.)

10. As the children enjoy the activities you prepared for the celebration space, emphasize that God himself is the greatest treasure. Help the children understand that God is such a great treasure, they

Notes

can have joy in him no matter what lesser things they give up as they walk along the path of life.

11. Thank God that he is the highest pleasure, deepest joy, and greatest treasure. Ask God to help the children know him as their joy and treasure.[13]

Notes

Options:

Offer specific opportunities for the children to sacrifice lesser pleasures for the greater pleasure of knowing and enjoying God as their treasure. Invite them, for example, to give away one of their toys so a missionary child who has left her toys behind while her family is on home assignment has something to play with on her long drives from one supporting church to another.

Review:

When God provides opportunities for the children to sacrifice good gifts, help them climb the mountain of God's perfect character to gain perspective, so they remember that God is a greater treasure than anything they sacrifice.

13 Noël Piper's *Treasuring God in Our Traditions* is full of inspiring ideas on how to treasure God as a family.

Section 2

Transformed

Transformed

We try and, when it comes to our children, we try harder. We poke, prod, and push them to do what they should. If we are spiritual, we pray—poking, prodding, and attempting to push God to make our children do what they should. The book of Romans offers a radically different way of living and parenting.

Our children were raised in the Deaf church. One day, our four-year-old son stood in our living room. He walked a few steps to his left, reeled over backward, and crawled to his feet. After repeating this process several times, he got up and trotted off to his right. When I asked what he was doing, he looked at me astonished. "Can't you tell?" he began. "I'm preaching in a Deaf church." He pointed to his left and said, "That's the way of the law. I kept trying and trying. I always got knocked down. Then, I went a new way. The way of the gospel."

Another of our sons was sick the first two years of his life. He cried often due to chronic pneumonia, bronchitis, and ear infections. His three-year-old brother told him, "Don't you know that people who believe in Jesus are dead to all that fussing and alive to praising God?"

We had wondered if our children understood any of the simple Bible lessons we had been teaching from the book of Romans. How we underestimated the Spirit's ability to reach the heart of a child with the beauty of the gospel! Those lessons are included in this section.[14]

Union with Christ, as explained in the book of Ephesians, is the foundation for every spiritual blessing:

> Blessed be the God and Father of our Lord Jesus Christ, who has blessed us in Christ with every spiritual blessing in the heavenly places, even as he chose us in him before the foundation of the world, that we should be holy and blameless before him. In love he predestined us for adoption as sons through Jesus Christ, according to the purpose of his will, to the praise of his glorious grace, with which he has blessed us in the Beloved. *In him* we have redemption through his blood, the forgiveness of our trespasses, according to the riches of his grace, which he lavished upon us, in all wisdom and insight making known to us the mystery of his will, according to his purpose, which he set forth in Christ as a plan for the fullness

14 Throughout these lessons, I am deeply indebted to Roseann Trott who taught me about my union with Christ by describing the Bible study she created for her children (which I have simply expanded in the lessons of this section).

> of time, to unite all things *in him*, things in heaven and things on earth.
>
> *In him* we have obtained an inheritance, having been predestined according to the purpose of him who works all things according to the counsel of his will, so that we who were the first to hope in Christ might be to the praise of his glory. *In him* you also, when you heard the word of truth, the gospel of your salvation, and believed in him, were sealed with the promised Holy Spirit, who is the guarantee of our inheritance until we acquire possession of it, to the praise of his glory.
>
> *Ephesians 1:3–14 (ESV, italics added)*

Many Christians, however, do not understand or apply this truth, which is the propulsive force of the Christian life. They do not help their children understand and live out their union with Christ. The gospel, with its promise of union with Christ, is the only lasting hope for children who explode easily, lament loudly, or fight ferociously.

Teaching children the commands of God without teaching them of their union with Christ short-circuits their growth in joyful holiness. Linger over these lessons from Romans 1–8. This is not a race through Romans, but a long, refreshing shower. A shower cleanses as one stands under its purifying water. Similarly, God's Word transforms those who put themselves under its cleansing cascade. I pray that these lessons will be showers of grace to help you and your children understand the power of the gospel to make people new and cause new people to do new things.

Teaching Tips

To most effectively teach the lessons, prayerfully read the suggested Scripture passage before teaching. Save all materials created or taken from Section 5: *Pictures to Download*; many of these materials will be used in later lessons. Any of these lessons can be divided into shorter mini-lessons to accommodate individual attention spans.

Lesson 30

Bad News

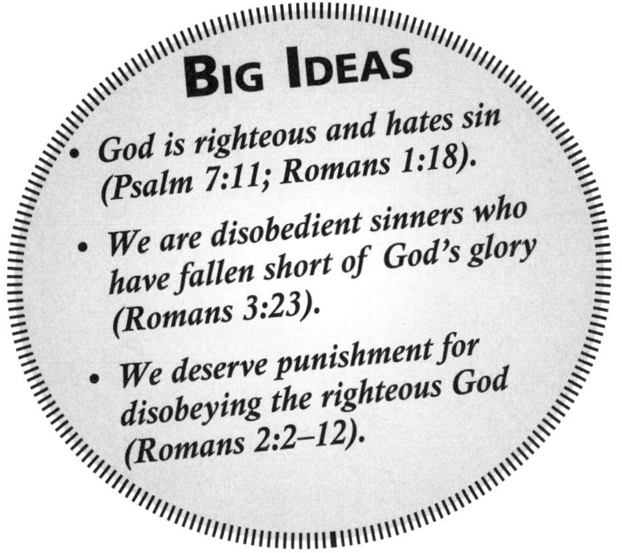

BIG IDEAS
• God is righteous and hates sin (Psalm 7:11; Romans 1:18).
• We are disobedient sinners who have fallen short of God's glory (Romans 3:23).
• We deserve punishment for disobeying the righteous God (Romans 2:2–12).

Scripture to read in preparation for teaching this lesson:

Romans 1:1–3:20

Materials

- Bible
- Paper lunch bag: swiped with mud (Dirty Bag)
- Container of mud
- Vinyl or nitrile disposable glove
- Picture-9 *Canyon* on page 273
- Picture-10 *Dirty Bag's Record of Sin* on page 275
- Download Picture-20 *Blank Record of Sin* and print for each child (see page 287)
- Optional: mirror and flashlight

Activity:

1. Pray that the Holy Spirit would teach the children about God's righteousness and their sin (John 16:8).

2. Explain that you are going to study God's Word from the book of Romans. Hold the dirty bag as if it is a puppet (with one of your hands inside the bag). Tell the following story:

   "This is Dirty Bag. God can see how filthy Dirty Bag's heart is, but we cannot. So, we are using mud to show Dirty Bag's sin. Dirty Bag was born dirty (Romans 5:12–20). Every time he sins he gets dirtier." (Using your gloved hand, put more mud on Dirty Bag as you mention specific sins that he does. Use some of the following examples, especially emphasizing those sins the children struggle with most often.)

Notes

a. God's law says we should honor God (Romans 1:21). Dirty Bag doesn't pay attention during worship.

b. God's law says we should give thanks to him (Romans 1:21). Dirty Bag complains about his food.

c. God's law says we should love him more than anything else (Deuteronomy 6:5). Sometimes Dirty Bag loves toys more than God (Romans 1:21–23).

d. God's law says not to covet—not to want other people's things (Exodus 20:17). Dirty Bag's friend has a new basketball. Dirty Bag wishes he could have his friend's basketball (Romans 1:29).

e. God's law says not to be malicious—not to want to hurt other people (Ephesians 4:31). Sometimes Dirty Bag gets mad and plans ways to be mean to his sister (Romans 1:29).

f. God's law says not to lie (Colossians 3:9). Dirty Bag often lies, hoping to avoid chores or discipline (Romans 1:29).

g. God's law says not to gossip (Proverbs 18:8). Dirty Bag loves to tell people about the bad things students in his class have done (Romans 1:29).

h. God's law says not to boast (Philippians 2:3; Romans 12:16). Dirty Bag loves to talk about how good he is at soccer (Romans 1:30).

i. God's law says not to disobey your parents (Exodus 20:12). Dirty Bag often disobeys his parents (Romans 1:30).

j. God's law says to "give thanks in all circumstances" (1 Thessalonians 5:18), but Dirty Bag complains about his chores (Romans 1:21).

k. Even though Dirty Bag does these wrong things, he criticizes other people for doing the same things (Romans 2:1–3).

Notes

NOTES

3. Ask the children to list the wrong things Dirty Bag thinks and does. Explain that the wrong things we think and do are sins. Help the children confess some of their sins.

4. Explain that God is righteous[15]—everything he feels, thinks, desires, and does is exactly what he should feel, think, desire, and do. Therefore, God hates sin and punishes sinners (Psalm 11:5–7). Ask what happens to people who continue sinning (Romans 1:18; 2:5). Discuss what should happen to Dirty Bag and each of you because of sin.

5. Give the children an impossible task by telling them to jump from one side of a large room to the other. Demonstrate how far each child falls short of the goal.

6. Show Picture-9 *Canyon* on page 273. Ask the children to imagine they have to jump over a deep and dangerous canyon. If they can not jump from one side to the other, they will die.

7. Let the children try to jump again. Explain that it doesn't matter whether one child jumps an inch or a foot more than another child; everyone who falls short of the goal will die.

8. Read Romans 3:23. Emphasize that each of the children is a sinner. There is a huge canyon between sinful people and the holy God. No sinner can jump across the canyon. Every sinner has fallen short and deserves to die.

9. Show and explain Picture-10 *Dirty Bag's Record of Sin* on page 275.

10. Give the children Picture-20 *Blank Record of Sin* (see page 287) and help them fill in some of the blanks. Do not be concerned if the children

15 This word is central to the book of Romans. According to Thayer's *Greek-English Lexicon of the New Testament* and *Smith's Bible Dictionary* (biblestudytools.com), the broadest understanding of the Greek term that is translated as righteousness involves the "state of him who is as he ought to be." Thus, righteousness involves being and doing what one ought to be and do.

underestimate how frequently and grievously they sin. For now, it is sufficient for them to recognize that they sin against the righteous God, fall short of his glory, and deserve his punishment.

11. Ask questions such as the following:
    a. Can Dirty Bag enjoy the friendship of God with his record of sin?
    b. Can you enjoy the friendship of God with your record of sin?
12. Save the children's records of sin for later use.
13. Review Romans 3:23. Explain that this is very bad news. In the next lesson, the news will get even worse, but then something very happy and exciting will happen to Dirty Bag.
14. Pray, asking God to teach the children how holy he is and how sinful they are.

Options:

1. If the children have not yet understood that they are sinners, prayerfully review this lesson until the Holy Spirit begins to convict them of sin.
2. To teach the concept of glorifying God, use mirrors and a flashlight.
    a. Explain that the light represents just the tiniest glimpse of God's glory. The mirror represents a person God made to reflect his light and show what God is like (Isaiah 43:7).
    b. Shine a flashlight so the children cannot directly see its light but can see it reflected by the mirror.
    c. Explain that people cannot see God but can see the way we reflect God's glory.
    d. To show that we are sinners who do not shine God's light and love, use mud to dirty the mirror so that it does not reflect the light. We have fallen short of showing God's glory and

Notes

have become like dirty mirrors who do not shine his light.[16]

Notes

Review:

1. Help the children memorize Romans 3:23.

2. Encourage them to find opportunities to apply it. When reading a book about a character who disobeys, for example, the children might quote Romans 3:23.

3. When the children sin, shape their consciences by explaining how they have broken God's law.

4. Use God's holy law to prime the children's hearts to cry out for grace.

5. Present the hope of the gospel by explaining that God's grace is available in Christ.

16 Taken from *Helping Children to Understand the Gospel*, which may be purchased at childrendesiringgod.org/resources/resource.php?id=3 or downloaded from childrendesiringgod.org/resources/resource.php?id=9&productPageId=2

Lesson 31

The Powerful, Powerless Law

Big Ideas

- We do sinful things because we have sinful hearts (Matthew 15:19). We need new hearts so we can be and do what God wants us to be and do (Jeremiah 17:9; Romans 2:29).
- God's righteous law can show us that we are bad/unrighteous. God's law does not have power to justify us—declare us righteous (Romans 3:20; Hebrews 7:18–19).

Materials

- Bible
- Dirty Bag puppet (from Lesson 30)
- Transparent plastic pump bottle (such as liquid soap dispenser bottle): filled with muddy water and set inside Dirty Bag
- Table
- Damp cloth
- Clear plastic bowl
- Aluminum foil
- Adhesive labels (or paper, marker, and tape) on which you have written common applications of God's law (examples given in lesson)
- Optional: red food coloring

Scripture to read in preparation for teaching this lesson:

Romans 2:1–3:20

Romans 7:10-24

Romans 8:1-11

Hebrews 7:18-19

Activity:

1. Thank God that his good law shows us how bad we are (Romans 3:20). Thank God that he covers believers with Christ's righteousness (2 Corinthians 5:21).

2. Review the story of Dirty Bag by asking questions such as the following:

   a. Is Dirty Bag righteous? Is Dirty Bag a sinner?

   b. What should happen to Dirty Bag?

   c. Are you a righteous? Are you a sinner?

   d. What should happen to you?

Notes

3. While Dirty Bag is upright on the table (with the pump bottle of muddy water hidden inside), continue the story of Dirty Bag by explaining the following:

   a. Dirty Bag is tired of being dirty. He decides to clean up his life. (Use a damp cloth to try to clean Dirty Bag, making sure to leave him looking even worse.)

   b. Every morning, Dirty Bag says, "Today I'm going to obey everything. I'm not going to complain. I'm not going to be lazy. I'm going to be good. I'm going to sit still, keep quiet, and pay attention."

   c. At breakfast, a box of Dirty Bag's favorite cereal has only a few stale crumbs in it. His mom says he can eat oatmeal, which Dirty Bag doesn't like. He blows up.

   d. Continue using real-life examples from the children's lives to show Dirty Bag trying to obey God's law but failing.

4. Explain that Dirty Bag does sinful things because he has a sinful heart (Matthew 15:19). Dirty Bag's heart—the part of him that feels, thinks, desires, and treasures—is sinful. Pull the pump bottle with muddy water out of Dirty Bag. Explain that this pump bottle represents Dirty Bag's heart.[17]

5. Pump some of the muddy water into the clear plastic bowl. Explain that when someone bumps Dirty Bag (hit the pump to dispense more muddy water), he blows up. The feelings, thoughts, and desires of his heart and the actions that come from his heart are sinful. When Dirty Bag doesn't get what he wants (hit the pump to dispense more

17 Romans does not speak of the old and new hearts, but contrasts the old self (6:6) with newness of life (6:4), slavery to sin with slavery to righteousness (6:16–19), and being in the flesh with being in the Spirit (8:1–11). The children I have taught have understood the heart as the part inside them that feels, thinks, desires, treasures, and functions as the control center for their actions. They have understood that they need new hearts. Because it is more difficult to communicate with young children about the self or the flesh, I have addressed those concepts with the old heart/new heart terminology that is used elsewhere in Scripture (Jeremiah 17:9; Mark 7:20–23; Ezekiel 11:19–20, 36:26–27).

Notes

muddy water), he gets mad and clams up. The feelings, thoughts, and desires of his heart and the actions that come from his heart are sinful. Continue with other examples that are relevant to the children's lives. Emphasize that the sinful deeds flow from his sinful heart. Dirty Bag can't change his sinful heart, so he keeps on sinning.

6. Wrap aluminum foil around the bottle of muddy water. Ask the children if the water that comes out of this cleaned-up bottle that looks so good will be clean now.

7. Pump some of the water out to show them that it is still dirty.

8. Put the labels (on which you have written those applications of God's law that children often hear) on the aluminum-foil-covered bottle as you show how God's law and other people condemn Dirty Bag. Pump out the muddy water as you say some of the following:

   a. Dirty Bag's mom says, "Dirty Bag, be nice."

   b. Dirty Bag's teacher says, "Dirty Bag, sit still."

   c. The Bible says, "Be kind."

   d. Dirty Bag's grandma says, "Dirty Bag, share your toys."

   e. Dirty Bag's principal says, "Dirty Bag, pay attention."

   f. Dirty Bag's dad says, "Dirty Bag, be quiet."

   g. "Dirty Bag, speak respectfully."

   h. "Dirty Bag, don't argue."

   i. "Dirty Bag, don't complain."

   j. "Dirty Bag, don't be a tattletale."

   k. "Dirty Bag, sit up straight."

   l. "Dirty Bag, work hard."

   m. "Dirty Bag, try harder."

   n. "Dirty Bag, love your sister."

NOTES

Notes

9. Show Dirty Bag feeling beaten down because of his sin. Show Dirty Bag feeling hopeless because he cannot change.

10. Explain that Dirty Bag goes to church (or school) and hears Romans 3:20, "Therefore no one will be declared righteous in his sight by observing the law; rather, through the law we become conscious of sin." Explain that, when God declares someone righteous, he justifies them so they no longer have a bad record of sin.

11. Dirty Bag understands that the law is good (Romans 7:12), but he is bad (Romans 7:24). Dirty Bag has become "conscious of sin" (Romans 3:20). Now he wants to be justified; he wants God to declare him righteous and get rid of Dirty Bag's terrible record of sin. Tell the children that God's law is powerful to show us what terrible sinners we are (make us "conscious of sin") but powerless to declare us righteous or justify us (Romans 7:10–24).

12. Help the children see that Dirty Bag needs a new heart.

13. Pray, asking God to give the children new hearts and help them live in new ways.

Options:

Instead of using muddy water, use water with red food coloring (since Isaiah 1:18 says our sins are like scarlet).

Review:

1. Help the children memorize Romans 3:20. Keep reviewing Romans 3:23 while learning this new memory verse.

2. When the children disobey God's law, remind them that God's law is powerful to show them how sinful (unrighteous) they are, but powerless to cleanse them from sin (make them righteous).

3. Cry out to God to give the children new hearts.

Lesson 32

The Best News

Big Ideas

- *Jesus always obeyed; he should have been blessed (Deuteronomy 28:1–14).*
- *Sinners are under God's wrath (Romans 1:18, 2:5). We cannot cleanse our bad records (Romans 3:10–20); we need a righteousness we cannot provide (Romans 3:10–30).*
- *Because Christ died for sinners who believe in him (Romans 3:20–25, 5:8), God justifies them—declares them righteous and gives them Christ's perfect record (Romans 3:21–26).*
- *The Holy Spirit gives the gift of new life (Titus 3:4–7).*

Scripture to read in preparation for teaching this lesson:

Romans 3:21–6:6

Ezekiel 36:25-29a

Materials

- Bible

Prepare in advance:

- Snack that can represent treasure (chocolate coins wrapped in gold foil or chopped fruit arranged in a paper box that has been decorated to look like a treasure box, for example)
- Moist bread that has been left in a dark place and is covered with mold: sealed in a transparent plastic bag
- Picture-10 *Dirty Bag's Record of Sin* on page 275 (from Lesson 30)
- Picture-11 *Jesus' Record of Sin* on page 277
- Dirty Bag puppet (as used in Lesson 31)
- Box (large enough to hide a clean paper bag and the Dirty Bag puppet): set up in front of the leader
- Clean paper bag: same color as the Dirty Bag puppet, propped upright in the open box but hidden from view
- Transparent plastic pump bottle (such as liquid soap dispenser bottle): filled with clean water and set inside the clean paper bag
- Clear plastic bowl
- Large cross (drawn on a whiteboard or made of construction paper, as used in Lesson 29)
- Tape
- Children's Record of Sins from Lesson 30
- Optional: small bottle of bleach; pump bottle filled with red water (from Lesson 31)
- Download Picture-20 *Blank Record of Sin* and Picture-21 *Jesus' Record of Righteousness* and print for each child (see page 287)

Activity:

Notes

1. Praise God for being holy. Ask him to teach the children God's good news for sinners.

2. Summarize the bad news of Romans 1:1–3:20 by reviewing Romans 3:23 and asking:

   a. Are you a sinner? Can you change your sinful heart?

   b. What does God's law have power to do? What doesn't it have power to do?

3. Give the children a gift—a snack that represents treasure. Before they eat it, ask if they need to pay for this gift. Emphasize that we do not pay for gifts because they are given freely. Show the children the moldy bread. Ask if they would trade with you, so you can eat their treasure snack, and they can eat your moldy bread. Thank God for the snack and for what Romans tells us about the treasure God gives to those who believe in Christ.

4. As the children eat their snack, ask if Jesus ever sinned. Explain that (1) Jesus never sinned, and (2) Jesus only did what was good and right.:

   a. Copy *Jesus' Record of Sin* (Picture-11)—the blank record that has Jesus' name on it and shows that Jesus never sinned (from page 277).

   b. Download *Jesus' Record of Righteousness* (Picture-21 [see page 287]) —with a tiny portion of the record of Jesus being/doing what God wanted him to be/do (John 4:34, 14:31). Explain that this would be just one page of Jesus' long record of righteous acts and thoughts (John 20:30–31; 1:25).

   c. Emphasize that Jesus never sinned and that he obeyed everything God says to do every minute of his life. Explain that Jesus is the only person who should be under God's blessing on those who obey (Deuteronomy 28:1–4).

5. Hold the Dirty Bag puppet as you continue his story:

a. Read Romans 1:18. Dirty Bag knows he has a sinful record and God is right to punish him.

b. Read Romans 2:5. Dirty Bag knows he is under God's wrath (God's righteous anger against sin). When he sins, he piles up more punishment from God. (As children who disobey, then lie about it, pile up more discipline.)

c. Read Romans 3:20. Dirty Bag realizes he cannot change his bad record. (Show Picture-10 *Dirty Bag's Record of Sin* on page 275.) He understands that he cannot make himself righteous.

d. Review Romans 3:23. Dirty Bag knows he cannot save himself. The next verse, after all that bad news, is the best news Dirty Bag has ever heard. Read Romans 3:24–25a. Dirty Bag understands that, when we have faith in Jesus (believe Jesus gave his blood and died for our sins), Jesus is our sacrifice of atonement. God's anger against our sin is poured out on Jesus and turned away from us. God gives us a free and undeserved gift—he justifies us (declares us righteous). Something wonderful happens: The Holy Spirit gives Dirty Bag … (drop Dirty Bag in the box) the gift of new life (pull the Clean Bag puppet from the box; Titus 3:4–7).

e. Clean Bag understands the bad news and the best news. He understands that he has fallen short of the glory of God. (He could never jump across the huge canyon between sinners and the holy God.) He knows that God made a different way to get him across the canyon. Bag's faith in Jesus' perfect life and death in Bag's place are like a bridge across the canyon between sinners and the holy God.

f. Read Romans 3:21. Clean Bag understands that God has provided a different way for him to be righteous.

g. Explain that Clean Bag has a new heart. Read Ezekiel 36:26a. Pull out the bottle of clean water. Explain that now, when Clean Bag

Notes

doesn't get what he wants (hit the pump to dispense clean water into the clear plastic bowl), the love and joy of Jesus can come out of him.

h. When Clean Bag believed in Jesus, something else happened. Read Romans 3:22. Romans 4:1–5:19 teaches that, when Clean Bag trusted in Jesus, God made a trade take place. Tape Dirty Bag's bad record of sin to the cross. Explain that God gave Clean Bag a wonderful gift: the perfect record Jesus. Write Clean Bag's name on Jesus' record of righteousness and place it inside Clean Bag.

i. Explain that the trade you offered at the beginning—trading your moldy bread for their treat—is just a tiny trade. Explain that trading a rusty bike with no wheels or handlebars for an expensive car is just a little trade. Explain that Jesus taking our sin, going under God's wrath on the cross, and giving us the gift of his perfect record, so we could be under God's blessing is the best trade in the world. It's the best news in the world, the best story in the world, and the best truth in the world.

6. Read 2 Corinthians 5:21. Thank God that Jesus was willing to become sin, so God could declare those who believe in him righteous. Thank God that Jesus was willing to come under God's wrath so those who believe in him could come under God's blessing. Explain that, because Clean Bag has the gift of Jesus' perfect righteousness/record (Romans 3:24), he can enjoy friendship with God forever.

7. Pray, asking God to give the children new life, faith, and the perfect record (righteousness) of Jesus.

8. Later, talk with each child individually to prayerfully discern whether that child desires to turn from sin and trust Jesus to make him or her new. If so, that child may ask for a new heart and put his/her record of sin on the cross. Give him/her a copy of the depiction of Christ's record with that child's name written on it.

Notes

Options:

To show the cleansing aspect of newness in Christ (1 Corinthians 6:11), use water mixed with red food coloring to represent the old heart. Pour bleach (representing the cleansing of the Holy Spirit) into the red water, illustrating God's power to make our hearts new (Isaiah 1:18).

Review:

1. Help the children memorize Romans 3:24 and recite Romans 3:23–24.

2. Help them see the connection between these verses.

3. Keep reviewing Romans 3:20.

4. Apply these verses to your lives.

Notes

Lesson 33

Joined With Jesus

Big Ideas

- *Those who believe in Jesus are joined with him (Romans 6:5): they are dead to sin (Romans 6:6–7) and alive to living God's way (Romans 6:4).*
- *Joined with Jesus, believers can do what they could never do in their own strength (Romans 6:1–14; Galatians 2:20).*

Scripture to read in preparation for teaching this lesson:

Romans 5:12–6:14

Galatians 2:20

Materials

- Bible
- Volunteers: parent, child, and helper
- Dirty Bag puppet
- Large cross (as used in previous lessons)
- Shimmering cloth, glued inside the Clean Bag puppet
- Materials for doing a particular skill (see below)
- Two (or more) bandannas

* Advance preparation: Prior to this lesson, privately ask a parent and child to prepare a demonstration in which the parent will perform a specific skill, using their hands, that the child cannot perform (sculpting, playing piano, etc.). This will be demonstrated in Steps 14–17.

Glue the shimmering cloth inside the Clean Bag puppet when the children are not watching.

Activity:

1. Pray, asking God to teach the children what it means to live joined with Jesus.
2. Review the story of how Dirty Bag was made new and given a new record by asking questions such as the following:
    a. How did Dirty Bag become Clean Bag?
    b. What happened to Dirty Bag's record of sin?
    c. What did Jesus give Dirty Bag?
3. Explain that Romans 6 tells us that, when Clean Bag believed in Jesus, he was joined with Jesus in his death on the cross.
4. Read Romans 6:6. This means that those who believe in Jesus are dead to sin (Romans 6:6–7).

5. Attach the Dirty Bag puppet to the cross.

6. Romans 6 tells us that, when Clean Bag believed in Jesus, he was joined with Jesus in his resurrection from the dead.

7. Read Romans 6:5. This means that those who believe in Jesus are alive to living God's way (Romans 6:4–5).

8. Explain that Clean Bag has the life of Jesus inside. We cannot see the life of Jesus inside people who believe in him. If we need an operation, the doctor who does the surgery will not see the life of Jesus inside our bodies. Since Clean Bag is not a real person, however, he has something inside him to help the children remember that people who believe in Jesus are joined with him.

9. Show the children the shimmering cloth inside Clean Bag.

10. Read Galatians 2:20. Explain that Jesus in a believer can do what that person by himself or herself could never do (Romans 6:1–14).

11. Give examples of Clean Bag doing new things because he is a new person who is joined with Jesus. Adapt any of the following examples to better fit the children's lives:
    a. Jesus obeyed God. Joined with Jesus, Clean Bag obeys God too.
    b. Jesus forgave his brothers and sisters when they sinned against him. Joined with Jesus, Clean Bag can forgive his sister when she calls him names.
    c. Jesus helped clean his father's carpentry shop. Joined with Jesus, Clean Bag can cheerfully clean his room.
    d. Jesus loved the children when they interrupted him. Joined with Jesus, Clean Bag can love his little niece and nephew when they bother him.

Notes

e. Jesus always trusted God. Joined with Jesus, Clean Bag can trust God instead of worrying.

12. Ask the child volunteer to demonstrate the particular skill that uses the hands and that you know the child cannot do: using clay to sculpt something that is not even in the child's vocabulary, for example.

13. Make sure all the other children recognize that this child cannot perform that particular skill.

14. Have the parent stand behind the child in such a way that the parent's arms drape over the child's arms.

15. Use bandannas to tie the child's arms to the parent's forearms. Explain that we cannot see faith in Jesus, but—as the bandannas tie the child's arms to the parent's arms—faith in Jesus unites us to him.

16. Now tell the child to perform the skill. Have the parent guide the child's hands to perform the skill.

17. Emphasize to the watching children that the child now performs this skill because she is united with her parent's arms.

18. Explain that this is another picture to help the children remember that people who believe in Jesus are joined with Jesus. The child performed a skill that she could not previously do because she was joined with her parent. As the child's hands partnered with her parent's knowledge and strength, she could do something new. Being joined with Jesus is different, however, because he teaches and changes us to work in partnership with him so we can do new things by his power.

19. Pray, thanking God for his power in making people new. Ask God to make the children new so they can do new things.

Notes

Options:

1. Read and explain John 15:4–5.

2. Use any of the following activities to either extend this lesson or replace the lesson's parent-child demonstration:

   a. Make an appointment to visit a local orchard or vineyard to see how one plant is united with another in the process of grafting.

   b. Watch and discuss one (or more) of the many online video demonstrations of plant grafting.

   c. Try grafting by following any of the many instruction guides available online.

Review:

1. Help the children memorize Romans 6:4.

2. Encourage them with this verse when they are tempted to sin.

3. Keep reviewing previous memory verses.

4. Use John 14:20 and Ephesians 3:17 to review and reinforce this lesson about the believer's union with Christ.

5. Review these truths often before proceeding to the next lesson.

Notes

Lesson 34

New People Do New Things

Big Ideas

- *Believers are dead to sin (Romans 6:6–7) and risen to new life (Romans 6:4).*
- *Believers have a new boss and do not have to obey the old boss of sin (Romans 6:14–19). They are able to obey God (Romans 6:13).*
- *Christians need to believe they are dead to sin and risen to new life (Romans 6:11) and act like it by doing new things (Romans 6:13).*
- *Christians give their bodies to God for him to use any way he wants (Romans 6:13, 12:1).*
- *Grace is God's kindness and his power to help new people do new things (Titus 2:11–12).*

Materials

- Bible
- Clean Bag puppet

Notes

Scripture to read in preparation for teaching this lesson:

Romans 6:1-23

Galatians 2:20

Activity:

1. Pray, asking God to help the children believe that the life of Christ in them can defeat sin.

2. Review the story of Clean Bag by asking questions such as the following:

   a. How did Dirty Bag become Clean Bag?

b. What happened to Dirty Bag's record of sin?

c. Who lives inside Clean Bag now?

3. Continue the story of Clean Bag, adapting the details to fit the children's lives. One day it rains, so Clean Bag can't play outside. His sister won't share her new toy. Clean Bag does not feel like a new person who is joined with Jesus. Since he knows Jesus will not take away the perfect record he has given him, Clean Bag thinks he can blow up at his sister. Clean Bag is about to blow up when his mother begins reading Romans 6:1 to him. (Read Romans 6:1.) Clean Bag's mother explains that some people thought they could sin since Jesus would forgive them anyway. Just what Clean Bag had been thinking!

4. Clean Bag's mother goes on reading. (Read Romans 6:2.) Clean Bag believes that the Dirty Bag he used to be is on the cross with Jesus. (Read Romans 6:5–7.) Clean Bag's mother explains this passage by telling the following story [18]:

   a. Mr. Sin was a bad man who stole children and made them work in his army. Mr. Sin told the children to do wrong things (like hurting people), think wrong things (like thinking it was all right to steal), and desire wrong things (like wanting money more than God).

   b. Mr. Sin called one of the boys in his army "Bad Boy." Mr. Sin told Bad Boy to steal money, and Bad Boy got caught. Mr. Sin did not care if Bad Boy died in jail. Bad Boy went before a judge named Mr. Law. Mr. Law said Bad Boy was guilty. Bad Boy would have to stay in jail until he paid a huge fine.

   c. A man named Mr. Lord came to the court. He wanted to adopt Bad Boy and make him a new man. Mr. Lord paid Bad Boy's fine, adopted him, and gave him a new name: John. Mr. Lord taught John about Jesus. He taught John that he did not have to obey Mr. Sin because he was now Mr. Lord's son.

Notes

18 This story illustrates the biblical concept of redemption—being purchased from slavery (as mentioned in Romans 3:24 and expounded in Romans 6).

NOTES

d. One day, Mr. Sin drove to John's home where John was playing outside. Mr. Sin yelled, "Bad Boy, get in!" John was so used to obeying Mr. Sin that he jumped into his car. Before Mr. Sin could drive away, Mr. Lord came out of the house and said, "There is no one here named Bad Boy. There is only my son, John, and he does not have to follow you anymore."

e. John remembered that he had a new name. He believed he didn't have to follow Mr. Sin any more. He got out of the car and ran to his father's arms.

5. Clean Bag's mom compares sin with that bad boss. As John followed Mr. Sin, we follow sin. It leads us into trouble and, in the end, death. Mr. Lord rescued John from the punishment he deserved; Jesus can rescue us from the punishment we deserve for breaking God's law. When we believe in Jesus, we no longer have sin as our bad boss. Jesus is our new boss. As John had to believe his father and quit obeying Mr. Sin, we need to believe that God has made us new and quit obeying sin.

6. Clean Bag's mother continued reading. (Read Romans 6:11–14, explaining each verse.)

a. Verse 11—John was dead to the sin that controlled him when he lived under Mr. Sin. He was alive to living in new ways under Mr. Lord's love. Counting yourself dead to sin means remembering and believing you are dead to sin. Counting yourself alive to God means believing you are made new, believing that new people do new things, then doing the new things that Jesus in you can do.

b. Verse 12—Sin is a mean boss who pays a terrible wage (Romans 6:23a). Jesus is the new boss (Lord) of everyone who believes. Because he took the punishment of those who believe in him, they do not get the wages they deserve (punishment forever) but receive the gift of enjoying him forever (Romans 6:23b).

c. Verse 13—Christians use their bodies to obey their kind, new master—Jesus.

d. Verse 14—Grace is God's kindness in making people new and giving them a new boss. Grace is also God's power to help new people do new things.

7. Clean Bag believes he is dead to sin. He quits complaining about the rain and the toy his sister will not share with him. Instead, he happily builds the best LEGO spaceship he has ever made. Clean Bag is putting the last block on it, when his sister runs through the room and falls—right on Clean Bag's spaceship. It breaks into hundreds of pieces. Clean Bag feels like hitting his sister, who is crying because she hurt her hand on the LEGO pieces. But Clean Bag remembers that Jesus has made him new. Clean Bag believes the old Dirty Bag died on the cross with Jesus. Clean Bag believes he is joined with Jesus. He offers his hands to Jesus and helps his little sister get up. He offers his mouth to Jesus and speaks kindly to his sister.

8. Pray, asking God to help the children believe they have a new boss. Ask God to help the children live as new people who do new things.

Options:

1. Children who struggle with motivation to obey may memorize Philippians 2:13.

2. Encourage them to confess the sin (of not wanting to obey) and believe that God can transform them into people who joyfully obey.

Notes

Review:

Notes

1. Help the children memorize and apply Romans 6:11.

2. After the children sin, ask how they could have thought and acted differently if they had believed they were new people who are joined with Jesus.

3. Keep emphasizing God's holy demand for righteousness and God's abundant provision of righteousness through faith in Christ.

4. Some opportunities for application include:

   Obedience: Jesus obeyed his parents. Joined with Jesus, children can obey their parents.

   Love: Jesus loved the little children. Joined with Jesus, children can love others.

   Speaking the Truth: Jesus told the truth. Joined with Jesus, children can tell the truth.

   Diligence: Jesus worked cheerfully. Joined with Jesus, children can do chores cheerfully.

   Worship: Jesus loved worshiping God. Joined with Jesus, children can worship joyfully.

Lesson 35

Secret Weapon

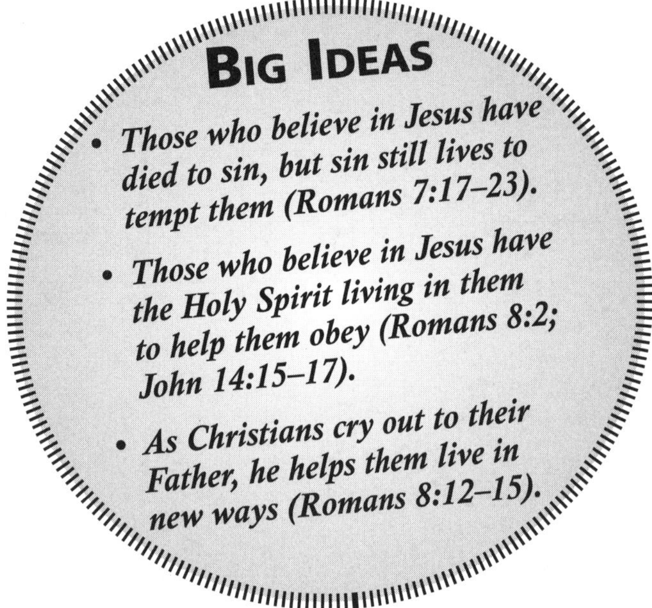

Big Ideas
• Those who believe in Jesus have died to sin, but sin still lives to tempt them (Romans 7:17–23).
• Those who believe in Jesus have the Holy Spirit living in them to help them obey (Romans 8:2; John 14:15–17).
• As Christians cry out to their Father, he helps them live in new ways (Romans 8:12–15).

Materials

- Bible
- Clean Bag puppet
- Desk or table
- Flashlight inside the Clean Bag puppet (ideally, this would be a flashlight that turns on with a quick touch)
- Transparent plastic pump bottles: one filled with muddy water and covered with foil and law labels (from Lesson 31); one filled with clean water (from Lesson 32)
- Filthy sock
- Download Picture-21 *Jesus' Record of Righteousness* (from Lesson 32, see page 287)
- Picture-6 *Four-Part Drawing* on page 267

Scripture to read in preparation for teaching this lesson:

Romans 7:1–8:17

Romans 8:26-27

Activity:

1. Thank God that those who believe in him are joined with Jesus. Ask God to teach the children by the power of his Holy Spirit.

2. Review previous lessons:

   a. The Holy Spirit made Dirty Bag a new person: Clean Bag.

   b. Clean Bag received the gift of the perfect record (righteousness) of Jesus.

   c. Clean Bag has a new heart that wants to obey God.

Notes

3. With Clean Bag upright on a desk or table and the flashlight hidden inside him, continue his story, adapting any of the details to fit your children's lives:

   a. It's another rainy day. Clean Bag was supposed to go outside to play, but now he's stuck inside and there's nothing to do. He wants to use playdough, but his mom (or teacher) says no. He gets mad at his mom (or teacher) and sticks out his tongue at her.

   b. Clean Bag is sent to his room (or the principal's office) where he is waiting for his "talking-to."

   c. As he waits, he wonders why it is so hard for him to obey since he's been made new. He expects his mom (or the principal) to tell him to try harder, love better, and control himself.

   d. So, when his mom (or principal) walks in, he says, "I'm going to try harder. I'm going to do better. I'm going to control myself."

4. Use the pump bottle filled with muddy water and covered with foil and "law labels" (from Lesson 31) to show again that the law has no power to change people.

5. Bag's mom reads Romans 6:2. (Read Romans 6:2.) She explains that we died to sin, but sin still lives. It still tempts us. That's why even people who are joined with Christ sometimes do the evil things they don't really want to do (Romans 7:15–24).

6. Hold up your hand with the dirty sock puppet on it. Explain that the sock represents sin. Show the sock poking and prodding Clean Bag—trying to get Clean Bag to obey it.

7. Clean Bag's mom reviews with him all that God has done to free Clean Bag from sin:

   a. The Holy Spirit made Clean Bag new. He's no longer Dirty Bag. He's a new person. Clean Bag needs to believe that Jesus has made him new.

   b. The Holy Spirit gave Clean Bag a new heart. Clean Bag needs to live out of the new heart

NOTES

that wants to obey God. (Show the dispenser bottle that represents the new heart.)

c. Jesus gave Clean Bag a new record—Jesus' perfect record that has no sin and is filled with all the good things Jesus did. (Show Picture-21 *Jesus' Record of Righteousness* [see page 287], then replace Jesus' name with Clean Bag's name.)

d. Jesus is Clean Bag's new boss. Clean Bag no longer has to obey the old boss (sin), but sin still tries to tempt him. Clean Bag needs to believe he has a new boss and not to follow the old boss of sin.

8. Clean Bag says this seems like a lot of work—believing and doing all these new things.

9. Clean Bag's mother reads from the Bible. (Read John 14:15–17.) Clean Bag's mother explains that God has also given Clean Bag a new spirit—the Holy Spirit. The Holy Spirit lives inside everyone who has been made new by God. The Holy Spirit is a powerful helper, to help God's children obey. (Turn on the flashlight that is hidden inside Clean Bag and keep it on for the remainder of this lesson.)

10. Explain that we cannot see the Holy Spirit, but he lives and shines in us. The light inside Clean Bag is a way for the children to remember that the Holy Spirit lives inside each person who has been made new.

11. Read Romans 8:14–15. Tell the children this means they can talk to God about anything they would discuss with a loving father. When they are tempted to sin, they can cry to God for help.

12. Tell the children that Clean Bag made a four-part drawing (Picture-6 *Four-Part Drawing* on page 267). Show the first part of his drawing in which Clean Bag is told that he can't use playdough, but can draw. Show the second part of his drawing in which Clean Bag is pouting and sticking out his tongue.

Notes

13. Show the third part of his drawing, which portrays Clean Bag praying, "Father, help me live by your Spirit as the new person you made me."

14. Show the fourth part of his drawing, in which Clean Bag is happily living as the new person God has made him to be as he creates his four-part drawing.

15. Thank God for the gift of the Holy Spirit, who helps us resist sin and obey God joyfully.

Notes

Options:

Children are often encouraged when they hear stories of their parents or teachers struggling with sin. Make your own four-part drawing, share it with the children, and pray together for the Spirit's transforming work in your own life.

Review:

1. Help the children memorize Romans 8:15.

2. When the children are tempted to sin, help them make four-part drawings, modeled after Clean Bag's drawings, but adapted to fit their situations.

<u>*Lesson 36*</u>

The Right Track

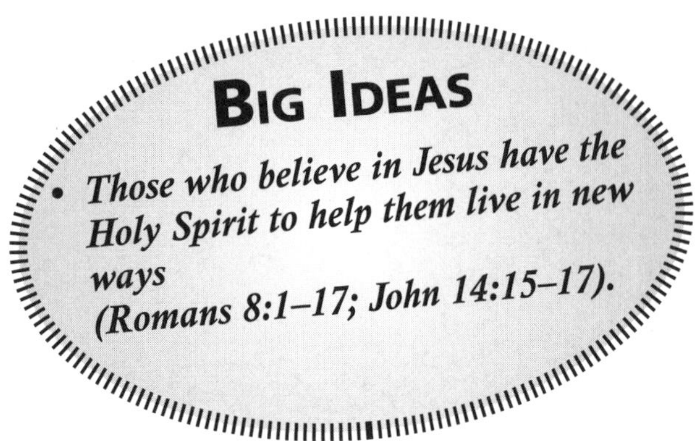

Big Ideas
• Those who believe in Jesus have the Holy Spirit to help them live in new ways
(Romans 8:1–17; John 14:15–17).

Materials

- Bible
- Train set or download Picture-15 *Train Engine* (see page 287), and homemade track (from Lessons 3, 4, 5, 14 and 21)
- Paper and pencil or marker

Notes

Scripture to read in preparation for teaching this lesson:

Romans 8:1-17

Activity:

1. Pray asking God to help the children live in the new ways of the Holy Spirit.

2. If using a toy train track, use a track splitter to make a **Y** track (as in Lesson 14 of Section 1, "Dealing with Feelings"). Otherwise, have the children make a train track that forms a Y. Write: *Old Way: Apart from Christ; Living by the Flesh* on one paper. Write: *New Way: Joined with Christ; Living by the Spirit* on another paper. Set the New Way paper on the right and the Old Way on the left side of the Y track.

3. Read the passages listed in the chart below and have the children pantomime the two different ways explained in Romans 8. For example, after reading Romans 8:1–4, have a child act the part of a condemning judge, wagging his finger and yelling, "You are guilty. You deserve to die." For its contrast, have a child act the part of a judge who goes beyond exonerating by declaring, "You are given this record of perfect righteousness."

Passages & Pantomimes Romans 8:1–4	Old Way	New Way
Judge pointing to grave; Judge pointing to a perfect record.	I am condemned.	Sin is condemned. I am justified.

4. Explain that, Dirty Bag was condemned, like a prisoner condemned to die for his crimes. Clean Bag is not condemned because Jesus was condemned for every wrong thing Clean Bag has thought or done, or ever will think or do. Clean Bag has the perfect record of Jesus. Joined with Jesus, Clean Bag does new actions. If the children believe in Jesus, they also have a new, perfect record, are joined with Jesus, and can do new actions.

Passages & Pantomimes Romans 8:3–4	Old Way	New Way
Machine unplugged; Machine plugged in and working.	No power to love and obey.	God gives me power to love and obey.

5. Remind the children that all the law labels slapped on the pump bottle (used to represent their hearts in Lesson 31) could not change the dirty water that came from Bag's old heart. Remind the children that the Holy Spirit gave Clean Bag a new heart. People who believe in Jesus also have new hearts. Remind the children that Clean Bag has a secret weapon in the fight against sin: the Holy Spirit. As Clean Bag lives by the Spirit's power and remembers that he is dead to sin and risen to new life, Clean Bag can obey God's law by loving God and others. People who believe in Jesus also have the Holy Spirit to help them fight sin. They are dead to sin and risen to a new life of love (fulfilling God's law). Christians do not wait for the Spirit to zap them so they feel love. Christians believe they are plugged into the Holy Spirit's power, then they love.

NOTES

Passages & Pantomimes Romans 8:5–6	Old Way	New Way
Child planning ways to disobey God; child planning ways to obey God.	Mind set on sin, which leads to death.	Mind set on what the Spirit desires, which results in life and peace.

6. Explain that, when Dirty Bag was angry about having to share a new toy with his sister, he planned ways to hurt her. Clean Bag asks the Spirit to help him think new thoughts. He thinks about how Jesus died so Clean Bag could love God more than any toy. Then he does new, loving actions.

Passages & Pantomimes Romans 8:7–11	Old Way	New Way
Child refusing to obey; child obeying her parents and enjoying special time together.	Hostile to God; not pleasing to God.	Submitting to God; pleasing to God.
Sea crashing on the Egyptians; Hebrew people on dry land.	Enemy of God.	Peace of God (Romans 5:1).

7. Explain that the Egyptians were God's enemies. We refused to obey God and were his enemies. When we believe in Jesus, we have peace with God. His Spirit helps us obey and please God.

Passages & Pantomimes Romans 8:9–11	Old Way	New Way
Dead, shriveled fruit, off the vine; fruit on the vine and bursting with life.	Dead in sin.	Dead to sin; New life in God's Spirit.

8. People who do not have the Holy Spirit are dead in sin, like shriveled grapes that are cut off from the vine and rot on the ground. People who have the Holy Spirit are dead to sin. The Spirit fills them with new life.

9. Explain that sin is such a bad leader that anyone who follows it will die. Clean Bag no longer has

NOTES

Notes

sin as his leader. Jesus is the best leader. He died to lead Clean Bag out of sin. He died so Clean Bag can follow the Holy Spirit. If the children believe in Jesus, he is their new leader. They no longer have to follow sin, because Jesus has set them free to follow the Holy Spirit.

Pray, asking the mighty Holy Spirit to work powerfully in the children.

Options:

This lesson may be extended by purchasing eggs, caterpillars, or chrysalides (in accordance with USDA transportation laws). No matter how many times someone commands them to do so, the eggs, caterpillars, or chrysalides cannot fly. In the same way, the law does not free the sinner's heart to soar to heights of love.

When the caterpillar has been transformed, it struggles—pumping fluid to its wings before it can fly. Christians struggle—fighting sin by the power of the Holy Spirit.

As Christians live by the power of the Holy Spirit, they do new things. Christians cannot fly, but Christians who believe they are dead to sin and joined with Christ by the power of the Spirit can do things that are as new as flying.

Review:

1. Help the children memorize Romans 8:4. Recite it often to strengthen the children's understanding of how the Holy Spirit moves Christians to obey.

2. Use otherwise idle moments (waiting at red lights in the car, waiting in line at school, etc.) to review the Romans memory verses.

3. When the children are tempted, remind them that the Holy Spirit is so strong he raised Jesus from the dead (Romans 8:11). Encourage them to believe that, if the Holy Spirit is strong enough to raise Jesus from the dead, he is strong enough to help them live in new ways.

Lesson 37

Adopted

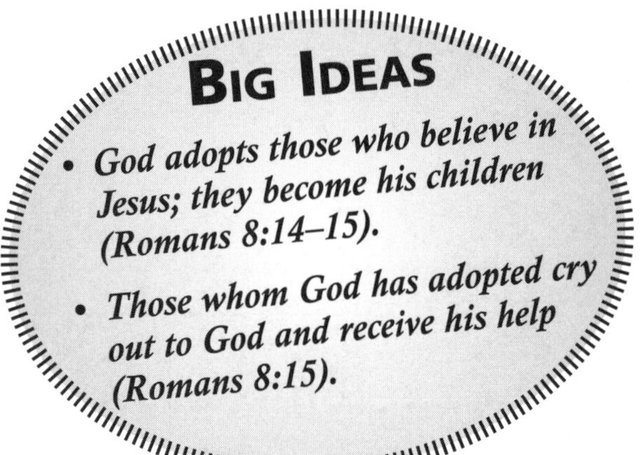

Big Ideas
• God adopts those who believe in Jesus; they become his children (Romans 8:14–15).
• Those whom God has adopted cry out to God and receive his help (Romans 8:15).

Materials

- Bible
- **Y** track (from Lesson 36)

Notes

Scripture to read in preparation for teaching this lesson:

Romans 8:1-25

Activity:

1. Pray, thanking God that he has adopted believers so they can be in his family forever.

2. Review the **Y** track from Lesson 36. Explain that any person God has made new is on the right-hand side of the **Y** track. Ask the children to listen to the following passage to find what God says about people who are on the right-hand side of the Y track.

   a. Read Romans 8:14. Explain that, when the Bible was written, sons had to protect each person and all the property in the family. So, males inherited the land and property when their father died. Now, females can be called "sons of God" because both males and females who believe in Jesus inherit all God's gifts.

   b. Read Romans 8:15. Explain that, when Bag was born, he did not have parents who could raise him. He lived in an orphanage. When Mr. and Mrs. Bag adopted Bag, they noticed that Bag was afraid of many things. At the orphanage, some of the older children had bullied Bag, and he was afraid of other children. Sometimes the orphanage did not have enough food; after he was adopted, Bag was afraid food would run out. Bag's parents taught him to call them Mom and Dad. They helped him to understand that they would protect, feed, and love him. Because Bag had been adopted, he no longer had to be afraid. In the same way, those who have been adopted by God call him Father and do not need to be controlled by fear because God cares for them.

c. Reread Romans 8:15. In the orphanage, sometimes Bag stole food. His parents taught him not to steal but to ask for what he needed. As Bag's parents adopted him and taught him to live in new ways as their son, God adopted Clean Bag into his family. God is teaching Clean Bag to call on him as Father and live in new ways as his child. Clean Bag can cry out to his Father for help.

d. Read Romans 8:16. Clean Bag and his parents went to court. Bag's parents promised to always love and care for Bag. The judge declared Bag to be their son and assured Bag that no one could ever stop him from being Mr. and Mrs. Bag's son. The Holy Spirit in Clean Bag is like that judge. The Holy Spirit assures Christians that they will always be God's children.

e. Read Romans 8:17. When Bag was at the orphanage, he did not own anything. When Bag's parents brought him home, they gave him clothes and toys. Bag lived in his parents' home and ate food that his parents provided. Bag became their heir and would someday inherit all his parent's money and possessions. Similarly, those who believe in Jesus are God's heirs and will inherit the riches of God.

f. When Bag's parents went to the orphanage to adopt him, they met other parents who were there to adopt a little girl. This mom and dad loved their new daughter and named her Hope. But, there was a paper missing from Hope's file. That paper would allow Hope to enter the country where her new mom and dad lived.

Notes

The parents adopted Hope, but they could not bring her home until they had all the right papers. Hope's mom and dad told her they loved her so much that they had adopted her, but they had to go home without her. They had to work with lawyers and courts to get the right paper. Then they would come back to take Hope home.

g. Even when her parents were far away, Hope believed she would go home with them one day. So, when children at the orphanage bullied Hope, she said to herself, "One day, I'll be in a home where I will be safe and loved." When food ran out and Hope was hungry, she told herself, "One day, I'll be in a home where I will be taken care of, and I won't be hungry anymore."

h. Read Romans 8:24–25. Explain that the little girl who had been adopted but not yet brought home had hope that her parents would do what they promised to do. That hope helped her wait patiently while she was bullied and hungry. The hope that she would go home one day gave her courage. In the same way, those who have been adopted by God know that he will someday take them to his perfect home. People who know that they will enjoy a wonderful life with God in a perfect place forever can be patient and joyful when they suffer here and now.

3. Apply these verses by giving examples of children who live as adopted sons and daughters of their heavenly Father:

   a. When a child is angry because someone else gets the first turn with a new toy, she prays, "Father, help me." She believes she is God's daughter. She sets her mind on what the Spirit wants: loving God and loving others. Then she is free to love God more than the new toy. She is free to love the child who is enjoying the first turn with the new toy.

   b. When a child is afraid of a thunderstorm, he prays, "Father, help me." He believes he is

Notes

Notes

God's son. He sets his mind on what the Holy Spirit wants: trusting God. Then the child keeps telling himself he does not need to fear because God controls the lightning and God loves him. He puts his energy into loving his sister and playing with her.

c. When a child is tired of doing her work, she prays, "Father, help me." She believes she is God's daughter. She asks God to help her work cheerfully. Then she sings while she works.

4. Pray, thanking God that his children are not orphans but have a wonderful father to take care of them.

Options:

The contrasting ways explained in Lesson 36 may be reviewed and expanded by adding the following distinction between the hopelessness of Romans 7:24 and the hope of Romans 8:24–25:

Old Way	New Way
No Hope Romans 7:24	**Hope** Romans 8:24–25.

Review:

1. Help the children memorize and apply Romans 8:16. Every time the children are anxious, they are acting like orphans. [19]

2. Remind them that God's children cry out to their heavenly father. Every time the children grab what they want (instead of asking God and trusting his care), they are acting like orphans (rather than acting like children who have been adopted and have the hope of going to a perfect home one day).

3. Remind them that they can trust God to take care of them.

19 I am indebted to Jack and Rose Marie Miller, who taught me to repent of living as an orphan and rejoice in living as a child of God.

Lesson 38

The Master and the Masterpiece

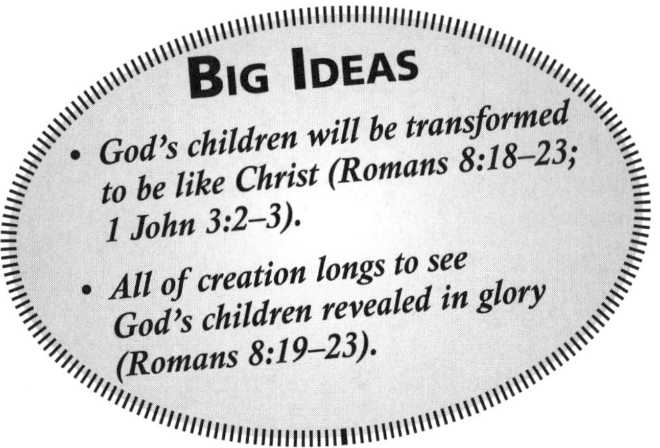

Big Ideas
• God's children will be transformed to be like Christ (Romans 8:18–23; 1 John 3:2–3).
• All of creation longs to see God's children revealed in glory (Romans 8:19–23).

Materials

- Bible
- Internet or books showing masterpieces
- Mirror
- Sheet
- Space (and any optional materials desired) for an unveiling

Scripture to read in preparation for teaching this lesson:

Romans 8:18-25

1 John 3:2-3

Notes

Activity:

1. Pray, thanking God that he is a master artist who is preparing a great masterpiece.

2. Explain that a masterpiece is a treasured work of art. Use the Internet or books to show famous masterpieces.

3. Explain that, before a masterpiece is shown for the first time, it may be hidden behind a veil. Elaborate preparations are made for the unveiling. Explain the following example[20]:

   a. Before the *Mona Lisa* was brought to the United States, French experts figured out how to safely transport it. It was kept in a specially designed case and carried in a special truck so it would not get bumped. Then it was put in its own

20 Taken from http://www.artinfo.com/video/president-john-f-kennedy-amp-mona-lisa and *Mona Lisa in Camelot*, by Margaret Leslie Davis.

locked room on a ship. Guards traveled on the ship to protect the painting.

b. American experts planned ways to protect the painting once it arrived in New York City. The painting was kept in a case that was the perfect temperature. It was put in a truck with Secret Service agents. Policemen and sharpshooters guarded that truck. Other trucks surrounded it. This line of trucks went through every red light to get the painting to the museum in Washington, D.C., quickly. The painting was not unwrapped until it was locked in a steel vault.

c. The most powerful, wealthy, and famous people were invited to the museum for the unveiling. The president's wife wore a gown that was covered with pearls. A band played the French national anthem and the American national anthem. Marines guarded the painting. Everyone gasped when it was unveiled.

4. Tell the children you will unveil a masterpiece (but do not let them know the "masterpiece" is a mirror). Help the children plan to carefully transport the masterpiece you have wrapped in the sheet to a special space where children can be brought later, one at a time, for a private unveiling.

5. Tell the children to listen carefully to understand what masterpiece God plans to unveil. Read and explain Romans 8:19–25:

   a. According to Romans 8:18, what is going to be revealed in believers? (Glory.)

   b. According to Romans 8:19, who is the audience at the unveiling? (All creation.)

   c. According to Romans 8:19, what masterpiece will be revealed? (The sons of God—all who believe in Jesus.)

   d. According to Romans 8:20–22, why is creation longing for this unveiling? (When sin entered the world, creation was corrupted. That is why there are destructive storms, fires, etc. Creation wants to be free of this bondage to corruption.)

Notes

e. According to Romans 8:19, what is the masterpiece that will be revealed? (The glory of the children of God.)

f. According to Romans 8:23, who else longs for this great unveiling? (God's people).

g. Explain the following: Remember the story of how Bag was changed from an orphan to a son when his parents adopted him? Remember Hope, the little girl at the orphanage whose parents had to leave without her until they could find the right paper so they could bring her home? Imagine Hope waiting at the orphanage. She would long to be with her new parents. She would long for her life to be transformed. We are like that little girl. God has adopted us, but he has not yet brought us home. We are in his family, but we don't yet enjoy our full transformation.

h. According to Romans 8:23, what do we long for now that will happen perfectly in the future? (The full transformation that will happen when God brings us home.)

i. According to Romans 8:24, what is hope? (Hope is being sure that God will keep his promises and joyfully waiting for him to keep those promises. Hope helps us wait for the day when we will be fully transformed so we can enjoy God forever with perfect bodies, perfect feelings, and freedom from sin.

j. According to Romans 8:25, how do we wait for this great transformation—this great unveiling? (With patience.)

6. Take each child before the veiled masterpiece. Tell the children that, if they believe in Jesus, they will be part of the great unveiling. Unveil the mirror so the child sees himself or herself. Tell the child that what he or she sees in the mirror now is not what will be seen on that day when God lifts the veil. What will be seen that day will be so beautiful that all creation will gasp at the beauty of each transformed child of God.

Notes

7. Pray with each child individually, asking God to help him or her hope in God.

Notes

Options:

1. This lesson may be extended by studying Ephesians 2:10, which explains that we are God's masterpiece[21]—created to do the good things God has planned for us.

2. Remind the children that those who are joined with Jesus are new people who have the Holy Spirit's power to do new things.

3. Great books can also be called masterpieces. In the Greek language in which the New Testament was first written, the Greek word used in this verse is *poiema* (which looks like the English word "poem"). Ephesians 2:10 says that each person who believes in Christ is God's *poiema*—a great poem or story written by God.

4. Brainstorm great deeds from the stories the children know.

5. Teach the children that God has written a great story that includes the new things he has planned for each of his children to do.

6. Encourage the children to believe that the Holy Spirit can help them do the new things God has planned.

Review:

1. Help the children memorize Romans 8:18.

2. Recite this verse together in challenging circumstances.

3. Keep reviewing all the memory verses.

21 New Living Translation

4. Every time one of the children is discouraged, return to this Romans 8 passage to fuel hope.

5. Make books that contrast current circumstances with what is to come in order to bolster hope and teach the children to consider by faith:

Current circumstances	Future circumstances
Creation Groaning Pictures from news stories or drawings portraying earthquakes, hurricanes, blizzards, pollution, etc.	**Creation Rejoicing** A wolf lying down with a lamb or calf lying down with a lion (Isaiah 11:6 or 65:25). Scenes from Revelation 21–22.
Bodies Deteriorating Pictures portraying physical deterioration—from colds to cancer, disabilities to death.	**New Bodies** Pictures of people with vigor for enjoying God and truths, from: 1 Cor. 15:35-55, Daniel 2:3, Rev. 21:4.
Temptation and Sin Pictures of people sinning or being hurt by other people's sin.	**Freedom from the Presence of Sin** Drawings portraying truths, from: 1 John 3:2, Romans 8:19, Philippians 3:21

Notes

Lesson 39

Transforming

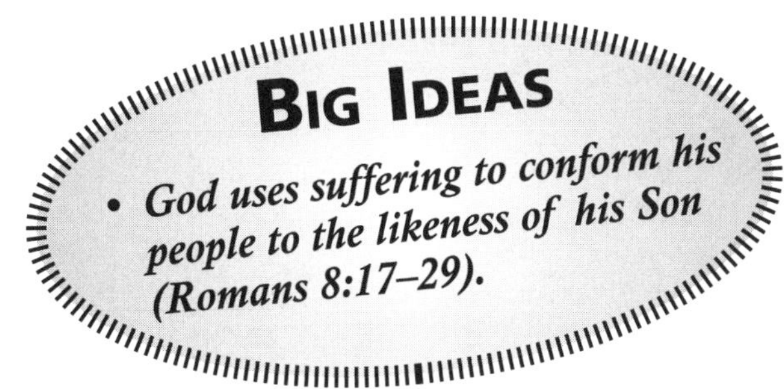

Big Ideas
• God uses suffering to conform his people to the likeness of his Son (Romans 8:17–29).

Scripture to read in preparation for teaching this lesson:

Romans 8:14-30

Romans 5:1-5

Materials

- Bible
- Model of a seesaw (may be made with blocks, or a board and box)
- Optional: small toy animal and large stuffed animal
- Clay, enough for the leader and each student to have a lump

Notes

Activity:

1. Pray, thanking God for the transforming power of the Holy Spirit.

2. Tell the children to listen to see what God brings us now to transform us into the people we will become. Read Romans 8:17. Explain that God uses suffering to transform us.

3. Tell the children to listen to discover what God forms us into. Read Romans 8:28–30. Explain that God uses our suffering—the hard things in our lives (sickness, death of loved ones, trouble getting along with people, etc.)—for his good purpose. God uses suffering to change us into people who are becoming more like Jesus.

4. Ask the children to listen carefully to learn why we can be cheerful when we suffer. Read Romans 8:18. Show a simple model of a seesaw. Ask the children what would happen if a mouse were on one side of the seesaw and an elephant jumped onto the other side. Encourage the children to imagine the elephant sending the

mouse so high into the air that it disappears. (If using toys or stuffed animals, demonstrate.)

5. Ask the children to imagine cramming every hard thing each child has experienced or will experience into a giant package, then setting that package on one side of a seesaw. The glory that will be revealed is the dazzling, beautiful, exciting, delightful things about God that we will share when we become like Jesus. That weight of glory is such a huge box that, if it were to fall on the other end of the seesaw, all the suffering each child experiences would fly off and disappear like the little mouse we imagined. All that suffering is nothing compared to the weight of glory that will be revealed in us.

6. Ask the children to imagine that the lump of clay represents Hope, the girl (from Lessons 37 and 38) whose parents came to her country and adopted her, but could not bring her home until a missing paper was found. Explain that her parents, before they left, taught Hope about Jesus. Hope now believes in him. Use the following examples (or examples from your children's lives) to show how God uses suffering to transform his children:

   a. Hope sees a girl with a pretty coat. Hope looks at her old jacket and feels jealous. She remembers that, if she were following her own way, she would go on feeling jealous. She asks God to help her think new thoughts. She looks at her jacket and thanks God that she has something to keep her warm. As you tell this part of the story, shape *eyes* in the lump of clay. Explain that Hope is learning to *see* God's gifts and be grateful. God is using the suffering (of not having a pretty coat) to transform Hope's *eyes* to be like those of Jesus, who *saw* his Father's gifts and gave thanks.

   b. During free time, Hope loves to draw quietly, but a little boy keeps talking to her. Hope is tired of listening, but she remembers that she is joined with Jesus. She believes she can do new things. Hope asks God to help her love this boy, then she listens to him. As you tell

Notes

this part of the story, shape *ears* in the lump of clay. Explain that God is using the suffering (of having to *listen* instead of enjoying peace and quiet) to transform Hope's *ears* to become like the *ears* of Jesus, who *listens* to our prayers.

c. Hope wants to be picked to walk to the post office to get the mail for the orphanage. Another girl, who just went to the post office, gets picked to go. Hope is angry and about to yell, "That's not fair!" She remembers that Jesus trusted God when he was not treated fairly. She believes Jesus lives in her. As the other girl leaves for the post office, Hope smiles and says, "Have fun doing such a fun job!" As you tell this part of the story, shape a *mouth* in the lump of clay. Explain that Hope is learning to *speak* words of encouragement. God is using the suffering (of not getting what she wants) to transform Hope's *mouth* to become like that of Jesus, who always trusted God and *spoke* words that honored his Father.

d. During play time, Hope runs so she can get a turn on the swings. She stops when she notices a little girl who is crying because she tripped over her shoelaces. The girl does not know how to tie her shoes. While Hope ties the girl's shoes, other children get on the swings. Now Hope feels like crying. Then she remembers that she has a new leader. She does not have to follow sin. She can follow the Holy Spirit. As you tell this part of the story, shape *hands* in the lump of clay. Explain that God is using the suffering (of sacrificing what she wants) to shape Hope's *hands* to become like those of Jesus. Hope asks if the girl likes to play soccer. They run to the soccer field.

e. Hope wants to score a goal today, but her teammates ask her to be the goalie. Hope thinks it is boring to be in the goal, while all the other children have fun running with the ball. She is about to stomp off angrily. Then she remembers that she has the secret weapon of the Holy Spirit. She runs toward the goal, imagining she is stomping out sin with every step. Hope loves

Notes

God and her teammates while she guards the goal. As you tell this part of the story, shape *legs* in the lump of clay. God is using suffering to transform Hope's *legs* to become like those of Jesus, who always went where his Father called him to go—even *walking* that hard road to the place where he would be crucified.

f. The lump of clay is being transformed to be more like Jesus, but it is not yet fully transformed into the glorious person who will be revealed when God pulls back the veil, and all creation gasps to see how beautiful the children of God have become. Explain that people who believe in Jesus are becoming more like him now, as they wait for God to bring them home and fully transform them.

7. Give each child a lump of clay. Ask them to transform the lump of clay by pressing it into the likeness of something new. Have the children explain their creations by saying, "I transformed my lump of clay to conform it to the likeness of a/an..." Draw parallels between the way the children transform their clay by pressing on it and the way God uses suffering to press on us and transform us to the likeness of Christ.

8. Pray, thanking God that he is powerful enough to transform his children to be like Christ.

NOTES

Options:

Study Romans 5:1–5, which also explains how God uses suffering to transform us.

Review:

1. Review the concept of heirs (from Lesson 37, Step 2e), then help the children memorize Romans 8:17. The children should now be able to recite, explain, and apply Romans 8:15–18.

2. When the children are upset, give them a few minutes alone with a lump of clay. Then review with them the way God uses suffering to transform his children, conforming them to the likeness of Jesus.

3. Help them see how God could use this suffering to make them like Christ.

Notes

Lesson 40

Unshakable

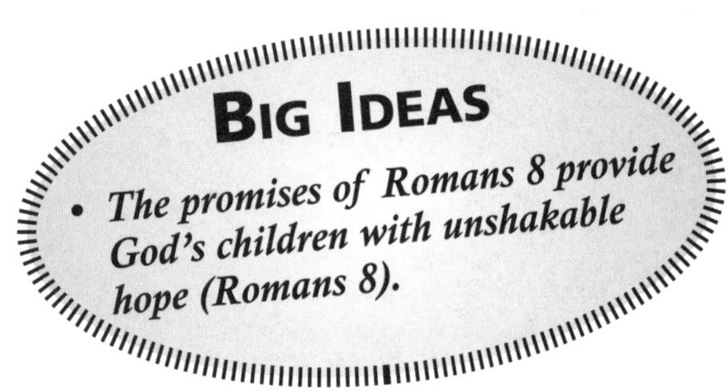

BIG IDEAS
• The promises of Romans 8 provide God's children with unshakable hope (Romans 8).

Materials

- Bible
- Materials for creating a castle (blocks, cardboard boxes, paint, etc.)

Notes

Scripture to read in preparation for teaching this lesson:

Romans 8:31-39

Activity:

1. Pray, thanking God for his great promises, which fuel our hope.

2. Create a castle. Explain that this castle represents the house of hope God has provided for his children as explained in Romans 8.

3. Read Romans 8:31. Explain that God is for every person who lives inside the castle of these Romans 8 promises.

4. Read Romans 8:32. Explain that God has given his Son Jesus, and every good thing that belongs to Jesus, to those who live inside this castle.

5. Read Romans 8:33–35a. Explain that people may say all kinds of terrible things about those who live inside this Romans 8 fortress, but none of those things matter because God has declared his children righteous. Jesus has paid for the sin of all who live in this Romans 8 castle, and nothing can make Jesus love them any less.

6. Read Romans 8:35–39. Explain that people who live inside this Romans 8 house of hope cannot

NOTES

be shaken. Nothing can separate them from God's love. Even though hard things may happen inside that house, nothing gets into the castle unless it comes through the door of God's love. The hard things that come through that door all work together for the good purpose of making God's children like Jesus.[22]

7. Pray, thanking God for the unshakable hope that belongs to everyone who believes in Christ.

Options:

1. Build a cross-shaped drawbridge for your castle.

2. Explain that those who are not joined with Jesus are outside of the castle. Those who are joined with Jesus have entered the castle by his cross. Everything that Jesus has as God's beloved Son belongs to those who live inside this house of hope.

Review:

1. As you do Section 3 of *The Gospel for Moving Targets*, keep reviewing and applying the verses the children memorized from Romans.

2. When the children are upset, help them interpret their circumstances in light of the hope that is theirs if they live inside the Romans 8 fortress.

3. Personalize Galatians 2:20 to review all the lessons in this section.

4. Help the children memorize and frequently apply this verse:

   I [and my sin of wanting my own way] *have been crucified with Christ and it is no longer I* [and my sin of wanting my own way] *who live but Christ* [and his desire to follow God's way] *lives in me.*

22 Adapted from *Future Grace*, by John Piper, pages 122–123.

I [and my sin of loving myself most] *have been crucified with Christ and it is no longer I* [and my sin of loving myself most] *who live but Christ* [and his love for God and other people] *lives in me.*

I [and my sin of laziness] *have been crucified with Christ and it is no longer I* [and my sin of laziness] *who live but Christ* [and his hard work for God's glory] *lives in me.*

I [and my sin of complaining] *have been crucified with Christ and it is no longer I* [and my sin of complaining] *who live but Christ* [and his joy and gratitude] *lives in me.*

I [and my sin of dishonoring my parents] *have been crucified with Christ and it is no longer I* [and my sin of dishonoring my parents] *who live but Christ* [and his honor to God and his parents] *lives in me.*

Notes

Section 3

Attention

Attention

This is what the Lord says—
your Redeemer, the Holy One of Israel:
"I am the Lord your God,
who teaches you what is best for you,
who directs you in the way you should go.
If only you had paid ***attention*** *to my commands,*
your peace would have been like a river,
your righteousness like the waves of the sea."
Isaiah 48:17–19 (emphasis added)

Section 3 of *The Gospel for Moving Targets* aims to help children and those who love them pay attention to the God who teaches what is best for them. Its goal is to help children find the peace and righteousness of Christ as they attend to the God who directs them in the way they should go.

This section is divided into three units. Unit 1 addresses methods and answers the question, "How should I pay attention?" When Jesus blessed eyes that see and ears that hear (Matthew 13:16), he was emphasizing the spiritual sight and hearing through which people respond to him and his Word. Those who respond with spiritual sight and hearing must first attend to God's Word with their physical senses. Children who are a constant whir of noise and motion have trouble attending to God's Word. Through God's might and mercy, these children can develop the habits that position them to hear God's Word and see God's beauty. These lessons help children put on attentive behaviors that flow from the renewed thinking they practiced in Section 2: Transformed.

Unit 2 addresses gospel motivation and answers the question, "Why should I pay attention?" By prayerfully stoking your children's gospel motivation, you are working in partnership with the God who sang over repentant Israel (Zephaniah 3:17). If the holy God can rejoice over Israel, he can help you celebrate your children's steps toward attentiveness. One reason God has given you inattentive children is to help you pay attention to his might and mercy in the gospel and fuel your delight in gospel grace as it works in your children.

Unit 3 addresses gospel power and answers the question, "How can I pay attention?" It points children to the power of transforming grace, the resources of the gospel, and the rewards of attending to God and his Word. It applies the principles of progressive sanctification to help children develop attentiveness to God and the authorities he has placed in their lives.

These lessons are aimed at children, but parents and teachers may find that they too have been paying attention to the wrong things, such as long to-do lists and how hard it is to accomplish anything with children who don't sit still, keep quiet, and pay attention. As you focus compassionately on your children, you can coach them *before they fail* with reminders such as:

> *"You will need to pay careful attention. How can you pay attention with your eyes? How can you pay attention with your ears? How can you pay attention with your hands and feet? Jesus always paid attention to God, and he can help you pay attention, too."*
>
> *"While we are doing this activity, everything you say must be on task. Give me some examples of off-task talk. What kinds of on-task things can you talk about during this activity?"*
>
> *"This is a silent activity. If you need help during this silent activity, what can you do?"*
>
> *"I'm going to tell you two things. Let's pray that God will help you hear and remember both steps."*

As you enjoy these lessons, may God give you the grace not to become distracted by discouragement. I pray that God will use these lessons to help you present your children with God's law: "...pay attention and gain understanding" (Proverbs 4:1b). I pray that God will also use this section to help you present your children with his mercy: "To the Lord our God belong mercy and forgiveness, for we have rebelled against him and have not obeyed the voice of the Lord our God" (Daniel 9:9–10a, ESV). May you persevere by faith—presenting your children with the grace that trains us to live self-controlled and godly lives (Titus 2:11–12).

Teaching Tips

Save all materials created or taken from Section 4 for review or use in later lessons.

LESSON 41

With My Whole Body

BIG IDEAS

- *Our bodies are gifts from God and must be used the way he says—for his glory (1 Corinthians 6:20). Paying attention with our whole bodies (Colossians 3:23) honors God.*
- *God calls us to pay attention to him (Hebrews 2:1) and tells us to honor our parents and other authorities (Ephesians 6:1–3; Hebrews 13:17).*
- *Those who believe in Jesus are joined with him (Romans 6). Joined with Jesus, believers can pay attention to God (John 5:19) and other authorities (Romans 13:1).*

DEVELOPING AND PRACTICING ATTENTION SKILLS

MATERIALS

- Bible

NOTES

ACTIVITY:

1. Ask God to help the children pay attention with their whole bodies.
2. Read 1 Corinthians 6:20. Explain that our bodies are gifts from God that must be used the way he says.
3. Read 1 Corinthians 10:31. Explain that God calls us to pay attention to him (Hebrews 2:1) and honor our parents and other authorities (Ephesians 6:1–3; Hebrews 13:17) by paying attention to them.

NOTES

4. Brainstorm ways of using our bodies to glorify God. Examples include:
   a. Loving, enjoying, and praising God.
   b. Running joyfully at playtime.
   c. Talking kindly with friends during playtime.
   d. Helping someone who has a need.
   e. Putting all their energy into keeping still and quiet when told to do so.
5. Read Colossians 3:23. Working wholeheartedly includes paying attention with our whole bodies. Illustrate the difference between paying attention and not paying attention by modeling behaviors that either exemplify or contradict the following:

- Heads:
  Brain, eyes, and ears on task.
  Mouths closed or talking only on task.
- Shoulders and backs straight.
- Hands:
  Folded or moving only as instructed.
  Raised to get permission before speaking.
- Legs still.

6. Tell the children they are going to learn a song to help them remember how to pay attention. The song answers the question, "How do we pay attention?" Practice paying careful attention while slowly making the following motions and singing the following words (adapted from, and sung to the tune of, "Head, Shoulders, Knees, and Toes"):
   a. "Head": One hand touches an eye; the other hand touches an ear; mouth clamped shut.
   b. "Shoulders": Touch shoulders and hold backs straight.
   c. "Hands": One hand raised.
   d. "To toes": Hands folded and body still from head to toe.
   e. Repeat c and d.

Notes

f. Repeat a–e.

g. "And eyes": Fingers move from near the eyes outward to point to the parent or teacher, as if indicating eyes tracking the parent or teacher.

h. "And ears": Fingers move from the children's ears outward to point to the teacher.

i. "And mouth": Fingers move from near the children's mouths outward to point to the teacher, to indicate remaining silent until talking is permitted.

j. "Even nose": Finger touches the tip of the nose.

k. Repeat a–e.

7. Read Hebrews 2:1. Explain that God calls us to pay attention to him and tells us to honor our parents and other authorities (Ephesians 6:1–3; Hebrews 13:17). Using our whole bodies to pay attention to God and other authorities honors God.

8. Help the children think of times when Jesus used his body to pay attention to God. Examples include Luke 2:41–52, 4:1–13, 8:19–21, 20:19–26, 22:39–46, 23:26–43. Remind the children that those who believe in Jesus are joined with him by the Holy Spirit. The Holy Spirit in the children can do what the children, in their own strength, cannot do: use their whole bodies and all their energy to pay attention to God.

9. Pray, asking God to help the children use their bodies to obey God by paying attention.

Options:

Make posters or bookmarks with visual reminders about paying attention with heads, shoulders, and hands to toes.

Review:

Notes

Review the song (from Step 6) during the following lessons as an exercise break. Review it before beginning other activities that demand attention. By practicing these behaviors, children can develop the skills and attitudes related to attentiveness.

LESSON 42

With Hope

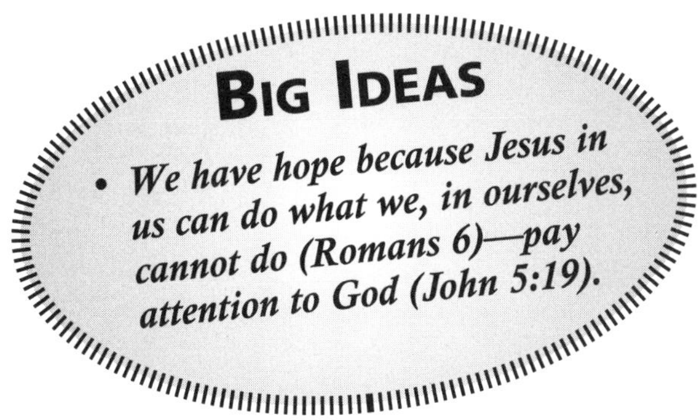

BIG IDEAS
• We have hope because Jesus in us can do what we, in ourselves, cannot do (Romans 6)—pay attention to God (John 5:19).

ATTENDING TO VISUAL AND AUDITORY INFORMATION; WORKING SILENTLY

MATERIALS

- Bible
- 2 objects and colored yarn or ribbons of similar (but distinguishable) colors
- Download Picture-22 *Simple Maze* and print for each child (see page 287)
- Optional: Download Picture-23 *Harder Maze* and print for each child (see page 287)
- Timer
- Optional: pencils, markers, crayons; paper

ACTIVITY:

1. Ask God to help the children pay attention to God with their whole bodies.

2. Review ways children can use the gift of their bodies to pay attention:
   - Heads:
     Brain, eyes, and ears on task.
     Mouths closed or talking only on task.
   - Shoulders and backs straight.
   - Hands:
     Folded or moving only as instructed.
     Raised to get permission before speaking.
   - Legs still.

3. Sing the "Head, Shoulders, Hands to Toes" song. Ask God to help the children be attentive with their brains, eyes, ears, and mouths.

4. Review concepts from Unit 2, Lesson 33:

   a. Those who believe in Jesus are joined with him (Romans 6:5).

NOTES

b. Those who believe in Jesus are dead to sin (Romans 6:6–7).

c. Those who believe in Jesus are alive to living God's way (Romans 6:4).

5. Jesus in the believer can do what that person, by him/herself, could never do (Romans 6:1–14; Galatians 2:20).

6. Show the children a string maze by placing objects to represent the start and finish points and arranging two yarns/ribbons of similar colors such that both begin at the start, overlap at least once, and have only one strand that reaches the finish. Have the children trace the correct path with their fingers without jumping from one strand to another. This step may be repeated with three strands of similar (or identical) colors. Finally, have the children track the maze using only their eyes.

7. Show the children Picture-22 *Simple Maze* (see page 287), but do not distribute copies yet. Read the beginning of Psalm 62:5, which is printed on the left side of the maze: "O my soul, wait in silence." Pause before reading the second half of Psalm 62:5, which is printed on the right of the maze: "… for my hope is from him" (ESV).

8. Tell the children that, after the next time you say, "O my soul, wait in silence," they are to remain silent until you say, "… for my hope is from him." Practice this step until the children wait silently for you to complete the verse.

9. Tell the children that, when you give them the maze, they should pay careful attention by following the lines using only their eyes and remembering which path completes the verse. Remind them that God can help them work silently.

10. Distribute the mazes, face down. Tell the children to turn over their papers. Say, "O my soul, wait in silence," and start the timer. Complete the verse when you think children have completed the

NOTES

maze with their eyes. If the children have worked silently for the few seconds needed to mentally complete the maze, celebrate the grace God gave them to be attentive and proceed to Step 12. If the children made noise, proceed to Step 11.

11. Stop the timer. Do not be discouraged if you have to stop the timer at one second. Rejoice that the children worked silently for a second. Pray for them. Repeat the timed activity and celebrate any gains.

12. Read the verse or have the children read the verse as they follow the correct path with their eyes or fingers. Repeat this step several times. Children may use pencils, markers, or crayons to mark the correct path.

13. Read John 5:19. Explain that Jesus always paid attention to and obeyed God. Explain that people who believe in Jesus are joined with him (Romans 6). Jesus in them can pay attention to God. So, the children do not need to be discouraged but can have a strong and joyful hope that Jesus in them can do what they could never do apart from Christ.

14. Thank God that Jesus never got sidetracked—never veered off the path God set for him. Ask God to work in the children so they stay on God's path without being distracted.

Options:

Keep this activity brief to encourage hope. If necessary, this activity may be done across several sittings/days. Two mazes are given, allowing you to choose the maze from Picture-22 or Picture-23 that is appropriate for your children and/or repeat the activity in order to reinforce the skills and concepts. Children may practice working silently and attentively by making mazes for each other (or you) to solve.

Notes

Review:

Notes

1. Keep asking God to help the children practice attentive behaviors.

2. Keep asking God to give you attentive eyes to catch the children being attentive.

3. Keep celebrating God's grace in the small steps your children take.

Lesson 43

By Hearing Treasure

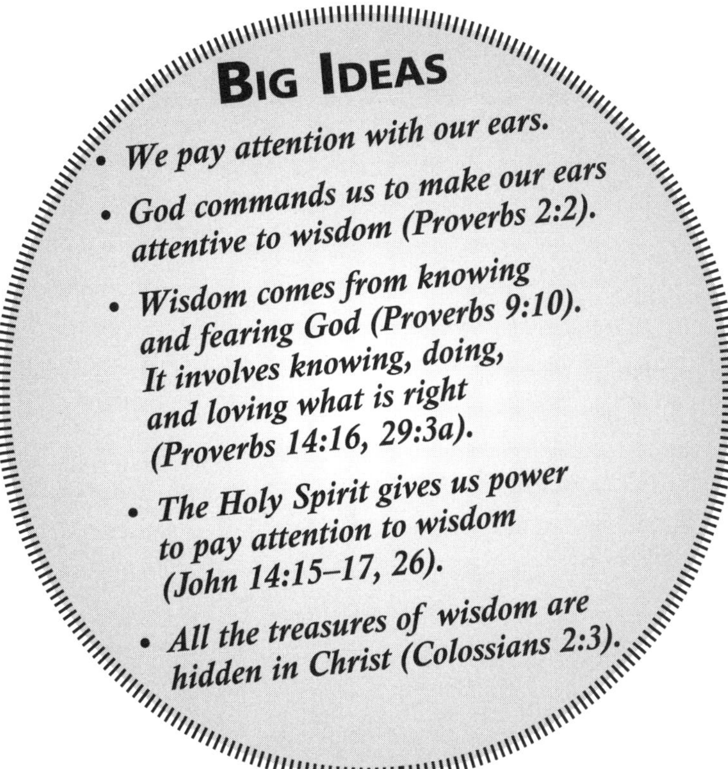

Big Ideas
• We pay attention with our ears.
• God commands us to make our ears attentive to wisdom (Proverbs 2:2).
• Wisdom comes from knowing and fearing God (Proverbs 9:10). It involves knowing, doing, and loving what is right (Proverbs 14:16, 29:3a).
• The Holy Spirit gives us power to pay attention to wisdom (John 14:15–17, 26).
• All the treasures of wisdom are hidden in Christ (Colossians 2:3).

ATTENTIVE LISTENING

Materials

- Bible
- Boxes (one per child) large enough to hold the cards or papers
- Materials to decorate boxes: markers, crayons, etc.
- Index cards or pieces of scrap paper
- Optional: picture books from home or public library (such as *The Indoor Noisy Book* and/ or *The Outdoor Noisy Book*, by Margaret Wise Brown)
- Timer

Notes

Activity:

1. Sing the "Head, Shoulders, Hands to Toes" song, then have the children sit quietly.

2. Review ways to use the gift of their bodies to pay attention:

- Heads:
  Brain, eyes, and ears on task.
  Mouths closed or talking only on task.
- Shoulders and backs straight.
- Hands:
  Folded or moving only as instructed.
  Raised to get permission before speaking.
- Legs still.

NOTES

3. Ask God to help the children keep their souls quiet (Psalm 62:5) and their bodies blameless (1 Thessalonians 5:23) throughout this activity.

4. Read Proverbs 2:2. Explain that God commands us to make our ears attentive to wisdom. We do this by paying attention to God and our authorities.

5. Read Proverbs 9:10a. Explain that wisdom comes from knowing God and honoring him.

6. Read Proverbs 14:16. Explain that wisdom means knowing what is wrong and turning away from it. Wisdom also means knowing what is right and doing it.

7. Read Proverbs 29:3a. Explain that wisdom means loving what is right. So, wisdom is knowing, doing, and loving what is right because it is pleasing to God.

8. Review the concept (from Unit 2, Lesson 35) that those who believe in Jesus have God the Holy Spirit living in them to help them obey (John 14:15–17). Explain that the Holy Spirit helps us to pay attention to wisdom, as Jesus paid attention to wisdom.

9. Colossians 2:3 says that all the treasures of wisdom are hidden in Christ. Tell the children that, as they pay careful attention with their ears, they will be able to hear treasures of wisdom in God's Word.

10. Have children decorate a box to use as a treasure chest.

11. Discuss the opportunities the children have to learn wisdom by paying attention with their ears: corporate worship, family worship, listening to their parents and teachers, listening to books, etc. Keep index cards or scraps of paper near the children's treasure boxes. As the children turn their ears to wisdom and find treasure, have them write

or draw reminders of what they learned. Put these in their treasure boxes.

12. Pray for the children to learn wisdom as they practice paying attention with their ears.

Notes

Options:

1. Read a portion of a picture book aloud without letting the children see any of the pictures. When the children have heard sufficient details, ask them what they remember. If you use books that discuss sounds (such as those listed under Materials), you can ask the children what sounds were mentioned on each page.

2. Keep rereading the page until the children have listed all the details. Then show them the illustration for that page. This activity may be done in several sessions or repeated with various books.

3. Use a timer to track the children's developing attention spans.

Review:

1. Focus your attention on praying for and encouraging the children's attention.

2. Coach the children toward better listening by alerting them and praying specifically for them before opportunities to gain wisdom by paying attention with their ears.

3. Regularly review the treasures of wisdom the children have stored in their treasure boxes.

Lesson 44

With an Undivided Heart

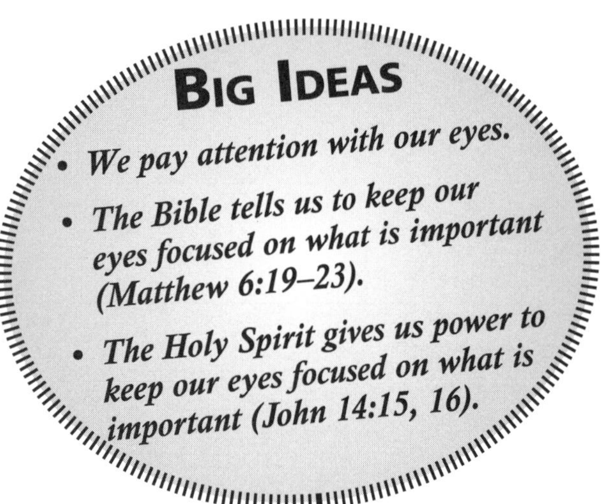

Big Ideas
• We pay attention with our eyes.
• The Bible tells us to keep our eyes focused on what is important (Matthew 6:19–23).
• The Holy Spirit gives us power to keep our eyes focused on what is important (John 14:15, 16).

ATTENDING TO VISUAL DETAIL

Materials

- Bible
- Oranges: at least one orange per child
- Download Picture-24 *Proverbs-2 Maze* and print for each child (see page 287)

Notes

Activity:

1. Review the "Head, Shoulders, Hands to Toes" song. Review ways to use the gift of their bodies to pay attention:
   - Heads:
     Brain, eyes, and ears on task.
     Mouths closed or talking only on task.
   - Shoulders and backs straight.
   - Hands:
     Folded or moving only as instructed.
     Raised to get permission before speaking.
   - Legs still.
2. Ask God to help the children learn wisdom by paying attention with their ears and eyes.
3. Give each child one orange. Tell the children to study their oranges silently. If any children make noise, gather all the oranges immediately.

Otherwise, let the children study the oranges for one minute before collecting them.

4. Mix the oranges so the children cannot track which orange was originally theirs.
5. Have the children examine the oranges until each child has found his or her orange.
6. Repeat this activity as many times as necessary until each child has found his or her orange after the reshuffling.[23.]
7. If some children struggle to find the right oranges, discuss reasons for that struggle and strategies the children can use to attend to and remember the details of their oranges.
8. Read Matthew 6:19–23. Explain that we cannot focus on things that are positioned in opposite directions. If we focus on seeing one thing, we will not be able to see the other clearly. Have the children try seeing things on opposite sides of the room (in such a way that it is impossible to see them both clearly at the same time).
9. Jesus goes on to say that we must focus our hearts on one thing: God. Give the children some examples of hearts that are divided because of trying to focus on two things: God and video games; God and movies; God and friends; God and toys (or other examples that apply specifically to your children).
10. Have the children practice visual focus and attention to detail by tracking Picture-24 *Proverbs-2 Maze* (see page 287) using only their eyes.
11. Practice this several times, reading the portions of the verses on the left and the matching portions of the verses on the right
12. Read Proverbs 2:1–5. Discuss ways Jesus obeyed this verse. Brainstorm ways the children can obey

23 I did not create this activity, but have borrowed it for so long that I cannot remember who did create it.

Notes

Proverbs 2:1–5 by turning their ears to wisdom (2:2a), applying their ears to understanding (2:2b), and searching for wisdom as for hidden treasure (2:4).

13. Read John 14:15, 16. Explain that the Holy Spirit gives us power to obey God by keeping our eyes focused on him.

14. Ask God to unite the children's hearts to fear and honor his name (Psalm 86:11).

Notes

Options:

If you review the puzzle page regularly, the children will easily memorize this verse.

Review:

We adults often have divided hearts. Sometimes we do not really look at the picture a child has drawn because our minds are distracted. Sometimes our children ask us to watch them do something, but we look away. Sometimes we do not hear what our children say because we are thinking about something else. When your attention wanders, admit to the children that you had a divided heart and ask for their forgiveness. Ask forgiveness for not honoring God by listening carefully to the children. When you cannot look or listen, simply tell the children that you need to concentrate on something else at that moment, but—when you finish that—you would be delighted to give them the full attention of your eyes and ears.

Lesson 45

By Keeping Silent

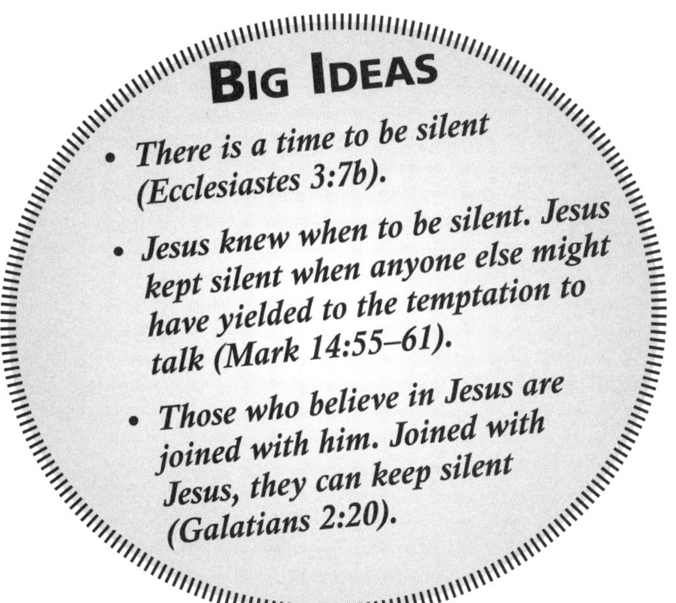

Big Ideas
• There is a time to be silent (Ecclesiastes 3:7b).
• Jesus knew when to be silent. Jesus kept silent when anyone else might have yielded to the temptation to talk (Mark 14:55–61).
• Those who believe in Jesus are joined with him. Joined with Jesus, they can keep silent (Galatians 2:20).

Materials

- Bible
- Download Picture-25 *Stars* and print for each child (see page 287)
- Crayons, markers, or colored pencils
- Timer
- Optional: coloring pages from the Internet or coloring books

Notes

ATTENDING WITH EYES, MOUTHS, AND HANDS; WORKING SILENTLY

Activity:

1. Review the "Head, Shoulders, Hands to Toes" song, then have the children sit quietly while you explain that this activity focuses on paying attention with their heads—their brains, ears, and mouths.

2. Ask God to help the children keep their heads, hands, and hearts focused on pleasing God.

3. Describe a scenario in which a group of mean people accuse one of the children of doing something wrong. Ask that child what she would do.

4. Tell the children that God says there is "a time to be silent…" (Ecclesiastes 3:7c).

NOTES

5. Explain that Jesus always kept silent when God wanted him to be silent. Read Mark 14:55–61. Explain that Jesus knew God wanted him to remain silent when he was wrongly accused (Isaiah 53:7).

6. Explain that people who are joined with Jesus have his power to keep silent when God wants them to be silent (Galatians 2:20).

7. Give the children Picture-25 *Stars* (see page 287) and instruct them to follow your exact directions as they color it. Tell them to work silently. If they finish before your next set of directions, they should sit up straight with their eyes on you, their mouths silent, and their bodies still. Time how long the children work silently.

8. Have the children follow these directions or adapt them according to your children's needs:

   a. Color the three-point star red.

   b. Color the eight-point star blue.

   c. Color the four-point star yellow.

   d. Color the nine-point star purple.

   e. There are two stars with six points. Color the six-point star with thinner points green.

   f. Color the other six-point star (with wider points) orange.

   g. There are two stars with seven points. Color the seven-point star with a circle inside brown.

   h. Color the other seven-point star pink.

   i. There are three stars with five points. Color the five-point star that is only a star (has no other shapes with it) black.

   j. Color the star that is inside another star green. Color the star around it red.

   k. Color the last five-point star your favorite color.

9. When all the children have finished coloring, compare their pictures to the directions. If there

are any differences, ask the children why they had trouble following directions.

10. Thank God for helping the children work silently and pay attention with their whole bodies, especially their heads and hands.

Options:

1. The activity in Steps 7–9 may be repeated often with pictures from the Internet or coloring books.

2. Read Daniel 6. Remind the children that God, who has the power to shut the mouths of lions, has the power to help them keep quiet when they need to be silent.

Review:

Adults also struggle with speaking when they should remain silent. When you say something rash, let your children see you ask for forgiveness and revel in the grace of the gospel.

Notes

Lesson 46

By Knowing the Time to Keep Silent and the Time to Speak

Big Ideas

- *God sometimes calls us to be silent and sometimes calls us to speak. (Ecclesiastes 3:7b).*
- *Jesus knew when to speak and when to be silent (Mark 14:55–62).*
- *Christians who are joined with Jesus can speak when God calls them to speak and be silent when God calls them to be silent (Galatians 2:20).*

Materials

- Bible
- Any picture book that is packed with visual detail

Notes

SILENT LISTENING; TALKING IN TURN; ATTENDING TO VISUAL AND AUDITORY INFORMATION

Activity:

1. Review the "Head, Shoulders, Hands to Toes" song, then have the children sit quietly while you explain that this activity focuses on paying attention with their hands and heads—their brains, eyes, ears, mouths.

2. Review ways to use the gift of their bodies to pay attention:

- Heads:
  Brain, eyes, and ears on task.
  Mouths closed or talking only on task.
- Shoulders and backs straight.

Notes

- Hands:
  Folded or moving only as instructed.
  Raised to get permission before speaking.
- Legs still.

3. Ask God to help the children pay attention with their whole bodies.

4. Read Ecclesiastes 3:1, 7b. Explain that God sometimes calls us to be silent and sometimes calls us to speak.

5. Read Mark 14:55–62. Explain that Jesus always spoke when and what God wanted him to speak. Jesus always kept silent when God wanted him to be silent. Explain that people who believe in Jesus are joined with him. Jesus in them can speak when called to do so and keep silent when called to do so (Galatians 2:20).

6. Show the children the picture book. Tell them to pay attention with their eyes and remember as much as they can from the picture. Let the children silently look at the picture until someone makes noise or until you tell them to close the book.

7. Instruct the children to raise their hands and wait silently until you call on them for their turn to tell something they remember from the page. Tell the children to pay attention with their ears because they must not repeat something someone else has already said.

8. Repeat Steps 6–7 as long as time and interest allow.

9. Thank God that Jesus always paid attention to God with his whole body. Thank God for helping the children pay attention with their eyes, their ears, their mouths, and their whole bodies.

Options:

Notes

This game may be repeated with different books. Another option is to ask particular questions such as:

- How many rooms were in the dollhouse?
- What was on the child's bed?
- What color was the truck?
- How many people were playing basketball?

Review:

Transitioning between times of talk and times of silence is an advanced skill. Adults also err by talking too much or not speaking when they should. Confess your struggle to the children. Let them see you going to God for forgiveness. Show them that you are with them in the fight against sin. Thank God that he is for us in this struggle and his Holy Spirit is in us to help us overcome sin.

Lesson 47

As a Living Sacrifice

Big Ideas

- *We worship God by offering our bodies as living sacrifices (Romans 12:1).*
- *Those who believe in Jesus have the Holy Spirit to help them obey God by offering their bodies as living sacrifices (John 14:15–16).*

Materials

- Bible
- Download Picture-26 *Butterfly* and print for each child (see page 287)
- Pencils
- Optional: pictures from coloring books or the Internet
- Download Picture-27 part 1 *Altar 1* and print for each child; download part 2 *Altar 2* (see page 288)
- Instructions for *Altar 1* and *Altar 2* are in *Options* on the following pages

PAYING ATTENTION WITH THE WHOLE BODY

Activity:

1. Review the "Head, Shoulders, Hands to Toes" song, then have the children sit quietly while you explain that this activity focuses on paying attention with their hands and heads—their brains, ears, and mouths.

2. Ask God to help the children offer their bodies to God.

3. Read Romans 12:1. Discuss ways of offering your hands to God as a form of worship:
   a. Drawing pictures that honor God.
   b. Writing words that honor God.
   c. Helping people in the home or classroom: washing vegetables, distributing papers, etc.
   d. Clapping while singing praises (Psalm 47:1).
   e. Raising hands to worship God (Psalm 63:4).

4. Discuss ways of offering your legs to God as a form of worship:

Notes

NOTES

   a. Running fast outside as you enjoy God.
   b. Keeping feet still during worship so everyone can focus on God.
   c. Moving toward other people to help and serve them.

5. Tell the children to focus now on offering their bodies to God by keeping their bodies still, and their eyes and hands focused on the work you give them.

6. Give the children Picture-26 *Butterfly* (see page 287). Instruct them to look at it carefully and draw an exact copy of it (without tracing it).

7. When everyone is finished, compare the children's drawings with the original, noting differences. Have the children redo their drawings until they make very close matches.

8. Pray, asking God to help the children offer their bodies to him every minute of every day.

OPTIONS:

This activity may be repeated any number of times with pictures of increasing complexity (from the Internet or coloring books). This activity may also be done as a silent activity.

The grid drawings in Picture-27 part 1 *Altar 1* and part 2 *Altar 2* (see page 288) involve more advanced attention skills. Have the children start at the dot and follow these instructions:

1. Beginning at the dot, draw a straight line that goes 10 spaces to the right.

2. Draw a straight line that goes down 6 spaces.

3. Pick up your pencil. Return to the dot but do not put your pencil on the paper yet.

4. Move your pencil 1 space to the right, then 1 space down. Then touch your pencil to the paper.

Notes

5. Draw a straight line that goes 8 spaces to the right.
6. Draw a straight line that goes 4 spaces down.
7. Draw a straight line that goes 8 spaces to the left.
8. Draw a straight line that goes 4 spaces up.
9. Pick up your pencil. Return to the dot but do not put your pencil on the paper yet.
10. Move your pencil 1 space to the right, then 2 spaces down. Then touch your pencil to the paper.
11. Draw a straight line that goes 8 spaces to the right.
12. Pick up your pencil. Return to the dot but do not put your pencil on the paper yet.
13. Move your pencil 1 space to the right, then 3 spaces down. Then touch your pencil to the paper.
14. Draw a straight line that goes 8 spaces to the right.
15. Pick up your pencil. Return to the dot but do not put your pencil on the paper yet.
16. Move your pencil 1 space to the right, then 4 spaces down. Then touch your pencil to the paper.
17. Draw a straight line that goes 8 spaces to the right.
18. Pick up your pencil. Return to the dot but do not put your pencil on the paper yet.
19. Move your pencil 2 spaces to the right, then 1 space down. Then touch your pencil to the paper.
20. Draw a straight line that goes 4 spaces down.
21. Pick up your pencil. Return to the dot but do not put your pencil on the paper yet.
22. Move your pencil 3 spaces to the right, then 1 space down. Then touch your pencil to the paper.

23. Draw a straight line that goes 4 spaces down.
24. Pick up your pencil. Return to the dot but do not put your pencil on the paper yet.
25. Move your pencil 4 spaces to the right, then 1 space down. Then touch your pencil to the paper.
26. Draw a straight line that goes 4 spaces down.
27. Pick up your pencil. Return to the dot but do not put your pencil on the paper yet.
28. Move your pencil 5 spaces to the right, then 1 space down. Then touch your pencil to the paper.
29. Draw a straight line that goes 4 spaces down.
30. Pick up your pencil. Return to the dot but do not put your pencil on the paper yet.
31. Move your pencil 6 spaces to the right, then 1 space down. Then touch your pencil to the paper.
32. Draw a straight line that goes 4 spaces down.
33. Pick up your pencil. Return to the dot but do not put your pencil on the paper yet.
34. Move your pencil 7 spaces to the right, then 1 space down. Then touch your pencil to the paper.
35. Draw a straight line that goes 4 spaces down.
36. Pick up your pencil. Return to the dot but do not put your pencil on the paper yet.
37. Move your pencil 8 spaces to the right, then 1 space down. Then touch your pencil to the paper.
38. Draw a straight line that goes 4 spaces down.
39. The children should now have a simple altar with a grate (show Picture-27 part 2 *Altar 2*), like those on which sacrifices were burned in the Old Testament.

Notes

Review:

1. Before entering a situation in which the children will need to be particularly still and/or attentive, pray together offering the children's hands, feet, minds, and whole bodies to God.

2. Remind them that Jesus can help them honor and worship God with their bodies.

Notes

Lesson 48

As an Act of Worship

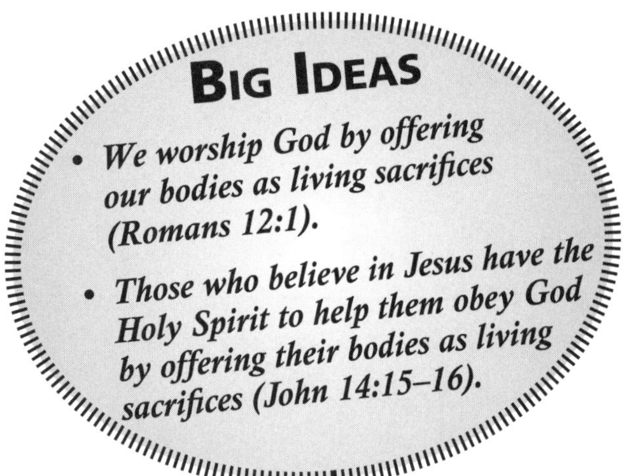

Big Ideas
• We worship God by offering our bodies as living sacrifices (Romans 12:1).
• Those who believe in Jesus have the Holy Spirit to help them obey God by offering their bodies as living sacrifices (John 14:15–16).

Materials

- Bible

Notes

PAYING ATTENTION WITH THE WHOLE BODY

Activity:

1. Review the "Head, Shoulders, Hands to Toes" song, then have the children sit quietly while you explain that this activity focuses on paying attention with their hands and heads—their brains, ears, and mouths.

2. Ask God to help the children offer their bodies as living sacrifices to God.

3. Review Romans 12:1; list ways to worship God with heads, shoulders, hands, and toes.

4. Tell the children to focus on offering their bodies to God by keeping their bodies still and their eyes and hands focused on the game you are about to play. Have the children sit cross-legged in a circle while you lead them through the following pattern of motions:

   a. Both hands tap thighs two times.

   b. Clap two times.

c. Fingers snap for two slow counts (so the children have time to name something on the first snap and point to someone on the second snap). If any children cannot snap their fingers, they may do another motion or fold their hands.

5. Practice this pattern until the children can follow it fluently.

6. Choose a theme such as animals, colors, fruits, countries, people of the Bible, etc.

7. The parent or teacher continues to lead the children through the hand motions.

   a. During the first finger snap, the leader names something that fits the theme. During the second finger snap, the leader points to one of the children.

   b. Everyone then resumes tapping their thighs and clapping twice.

   c. During the next finger snap, the child who was selected must name something else that fits the theme. During the following finger snap, that child points to another participant.

8. Continue following this pattern:
   Once children are skilled at this game, increase the demand for attention by:

   a. Increasing the pace.

   b. Having children who make mistakes sit out until one champion is left.

9. Mistakes include:

   a. Breaking the rhythm by not naming something that fits the theme during the first finger snap.

   b. Naming something that clearly does not fit the category.

   c. Naming something that has already been said.

   d. Forgetting to point to another participant on the second finger snap.

NOTES

10. Remind the children that those who believe in Jesus have the Holy Spirit to help them obey God by offering their bodies as living sacrifices (John 14:5–6).

11. Pray, thanking God for his powerful Holy Spirit and asking the Spirit to help the children offer their bodies as living sacrifices to God.

Notes

Options:

1. The game may be simplified by having children give their word during the claps (instead of during the first snap) and point to another participant during the snaps.

2. The game may be varied by having each participant choose a word that fits a certain theme before beginning the taps, claps, and snaps. After the children have announced their word choice, the game begins. Each participant must then give her own word during the first finger snap, and a fellow participant's word during the second finger snap. The person whose word was given then repeats the process. This option works well with vocabulary words from second languages the children are studying.

Review:

1. As you read the Bible, point out ways Jesus used his body to worship and honor God. Thank God often for the ways the children use their bodies to serve God.

2. Before worship, review Romans 12:1 and remind the children of the opportunities they will have to worship God by offering their bodies as living sacrifices.

3. Pray for them, asking God to help them offer to him their eyes as they focus on the sacraments, the music, and the Bible.

4. Ask God to help them offer to him their ears as they listen to the Word as it is read, prayed, sung, and preached.

5. Ask God to help them offer to him their minds as they think about God and his Word.

6. Ask God to help them offer to him their hands as they give money, fold them in prayer, or raise them in praise.

7. Ask God to help them offer to him their whole bodies as they sit still, so they (and other people) can focus on God.

Notes

LESSON 49

With Eyes on Jesus

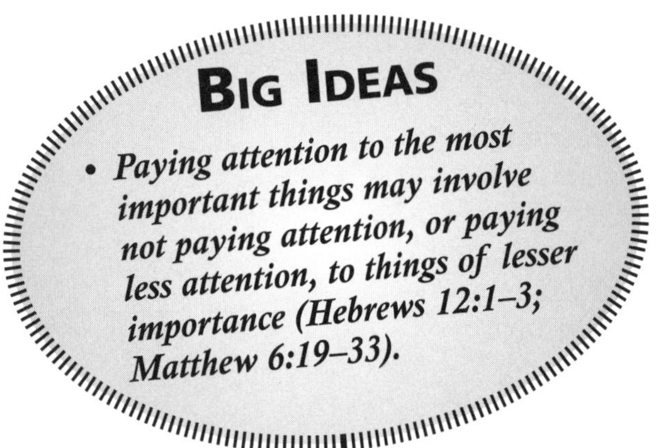

BIG IDEAS
• Paying attention to the most important things may involve not paying attention, or paying less attention, to things of lesser importance (Hebrews 12:1–3; Matthew 6:19–33).

ATTENDING TO DETAIL

MATERIALS

- Bible
- Download Picture-28 *Jesus and Lamb* (see page 288) and print for each child
- Download Picture-29 *Doesn't Belong?* (see page 288) and print for each child
- Pencils and paper
- Optional: cardboard tubes (one per child) from paper towel or toilet paper rolls

ACTIVITY:

1. Review the "Head, Shoulders, Hands to Toes" song, then have the children sit quietly while you explain that this activity focuses on paying attention with their hands and heads—their brains, ears, and mouths.

2. Ask God to help the children keep their eyes on Jesus Christ.

3. Read and discuss Hebrews 12:1–3.

4. Give each child Picture-28 *Jesus and Lamb* (see page 288). Make sure the children keep the picture oriented according to the "Top" and "Bottom" labels. Point out the letters **J e s u s**. Tell the children to focus on those letters while copying each line of the drawing as exactly as they can.

5. After the children finish their copies, have them turn the original picture and their copy upside down to see the picture of Jesus. Discuss the way that focusing on the letters **J e s u s** helped the children draw more accurately.

NOTES

6. Brainstorm ways of keeping the eyes of their hearts on Jesus.

7. Reread Hebrews 12:1–3. Discuss what Jesus paid attention to while he was on the cross. Discuss what Jesus did not pay attention to on the cross.

8. Have the children stand still and look at as much of the room as they can, straining to catch as much as possible with their peripheral vision.

9. Now have the children put their hands on either side of their eyes (blocking their peripheral vision). Discuss how this changes the way they see. Which way of seeing makes a central object most clear?

10. Give the children Picture-29 *Doesn't Belong?* (see page 288). Discuss the example and help the children see that thoughts about the Bible, praising God, and the cross belong during times of worship, but angry thoughts of revenge do not belong (are "off-task").

11. Have the children complete the activity page, then discuss their answers.

12. Ask God to help the children focus on the joy that comes from obeying God.

13. Thank God that Jesus always kept his eyes on God. People who believe in him have Jesus, with his single-hearted focus, living within them (Galatians 2:20).

Options:

1. Discuss what can happen to runners who take their eyes off the finish line and look at their competitors. Children (and adults) are often distracted by other people's sin. Encourage the children to pray for those who sin against them, but not to let other people's sin take them off course. Encourage them to keep their eyes on Jesus, not on other people.

Notes

2. Children may make *Which of These Things Do Not Belong?* activity pages (like the one done in Step 10) by drawing four items such that one item does not belong. Children may then exchange pages and figure out which items do not belong.

3. Look at the night sky on a clear night. Then look through a cardboard tube (from paper towels or toilet paper). Note how looking through the tube focuses your field of vision to make the stars appear brighter. Ask God to help the children focus on Jesus so they can better see his brightness.

Review:

1. Every sin involves setting our eyes or hearts on something other than Jesus. When the children sin, ask them what they were setting their hearts on, or what they were thinking about, that seemed more important than Jesus.

2. Pray Proverbs 17:24 for the children, asking God to help them keep wisdom in view, rather than being like fools whose eyes wander everywhere.

Notes

Lesson 50

By Running the Race

Big Ideas

- *Paying attention to the most important things may involve not paying attention, or paying less attention, to things of lesser importance (Hebrews 12:1; Matthew 6:19–33).*
- *Jesus gave up good gifts for better things (Luke 6:12). Joined with Jesus (Galatians 2:20), the children can give up good gifts for better things.*

Materials

- Bible
- Backpacks filled with things the children enjoy (toys, books, DVDs, etc.)
- Optional: timer

Notes

LISTENING ATTENTIVELY

Activity:

1. Review the "Head, Shoulders, Hands to Toes" song, then have the children sit quietly while you explain that this activity focuses on paying attention with their hands and heads—their brains, ears, and mouths.

2. Pray that the children will learn to cry out to God for help and power when they are distracted.

3. Read Hebrews 12:1. Explain that the Christian life is like a race.

4. Let the children put on a heavy backpack that is stuffed with toys, books, DVDs, or other things the children enjoy. (Make sure the backpack is not heavy enough to cause injury.)

5. Explain the rules for any race that is appropriate for the children's ability level. Have the children attempt the race while they are weighed down with the backpack.

6. Let the children (carefully) throw off the weight that is hindering them, then redo the physical activity.

7. Have the children explain which effort was easier and why.

8. Read Hebrews 12:1. Explain that some things, even though they may be good things, can weigh us down and make it hard to run fast.

9. As you unpack the backpacks, explain how each good gift can weigh us down, making it hard to joyfully run the race of the Christian life. Examples include:

    a. Reading other books instead of reading the Bible keeps us from enjoying God's Word and running the race of the Christian life well.

    b. Playing with toys can distract us from God, so we don't run the race of the Christian life well.

    c. Watching movies and television instead of enjoying family worship can keep us from running the race of the Christian life well.

10. Read Hebrews 12:1 and/or Matthew 6:19–33. Explain that paying attention to the most important things may involve not paying attention, or paying less attention, to things of lesser importance.

11. Read Luke 6:12. Ask what good gift this shows Jesus giving up in order to run his race well (sleep). Remind the children that Jesus in them can do what does not come naturally to them—giving up good things for better things.

12. Demonstrate the difference between holding something with an open hand and a closed fist. Allow the children to see which is effective: letting go of an item when your hand is open or when

NOTES

your fist is closed. Encourage the children to hold toys, books, movies, friends, and other gifts from God with an open hand, rather than a closed fist.

13. Explain that Jesus held God's gifts with an open hand. Jesus gives his people power to hold things with an open hand.

14. Pray that the children would joyfully run the race God has marked out for each of them. Ask God to make them willing to give up things that are weighing them down and distracting them from God.

Notes

Options:

1. Teach the children about inordinate desires by reading and discussing James 4:1–2 and 1:14–15. Lead them in repenting when good gifts become inordinate desires.

2. Time the children as they do Steps 4–6 to see if there is a measurable difference.

3. Watch or read about racers, discussing the design of their clothing. Competitive downhill skiers may wear seamless ski suits to reduce wind resistance. To minimize drag, competitive sprinters wear suits with "dimples," and swimmers wear streamlined suits that are water-resistant. Make applications to Hebrews 12:1 and the children's lives.

Review:

1. Look for opportunities to practice giving up good things in order to be able to race well: not playing video games in order to help neighbors, not watching movies in order to enjoy family worship, etc.

2. Remind the children to hold God's gifts with open hands, not clenched fists. When the children suffer losses, pray that they will hold God's gifts with open hands, not clenched fists.

3. When the children have emotional upsets, read James 4:1–4 and trace the path from the inordinate desires they allowed to control them to their sinful actions.[24] For example, help children to see that their argument stemmed from both wanting the same toy more than they wanted to honor and enjoy God and love each other. Because they desired that toy more than God (holding it with a clenched fist, rather than an open hand), they called each other names and exchanged blows.

4. Pray with them, asking God to help them to treasure Christ more than anything else.

NOTES

24 For more on the topic of inordinate desires leading to sin, see Chapter 5 of *Instruments in the Redeemer's Hands,* by Paul David Tripp.

Lesson 51

By Throwing off Sin

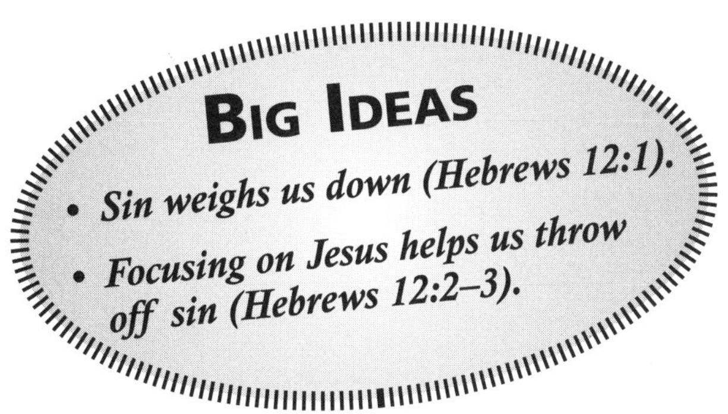

BIG IDEAS
• Sin weighs us down (Hebrews 12:1).
• Focusing on Jesus helps us throw off sin (Hebrews 12:2–3).

Materials

- Bible
- Backpacks labeled "Sin"
- Weights: brick(s), rock(s), etc.

Notes

LISTENING ATTENTIVELY

Activity:

1. Review the "Head, Shoulders, Hands to Toes" song, then have the children sit quietly while you explain that this activity focuses on paying attention with their hands and heads—their brains, ears, and mouths.

2. Review ways to use the gift of their bodies to pay attention:

- Heads:
  Brain, eyes, and ears on task.
  Mouths closed or talking only on task.
  Shoulders and backs straight.
- Hands:
  Folded or moving only as instructed.
  Raised to get permission before speaking.
- Legs still.

3. Pray that the children will learn to cry out to God for help and power when they are weighed down by sin.

4. Read and discuss Hebrews 12:1.

5. Put bricks in the backpacks (without weighting them enough to cause injury). Label the backpacks "Sin."

6. Have the children wear the backpacks while doing a physical challenge, such as running a set distance.

7. Repeat the activity done in Step 6 without the weights. Have the children explain which activity was easier and discuss ways sin keeps us from running well.

    a. Fighting with a friend or sibling over a toy, instead of working out a peaceful plan for sharing the toy, takes you off course and slows down your race.

    b. Playing with toys, when you have been told to put them away, takes you off course and slows down your race.

8. Read and discuss Hebrews 12:2–3. Brainstorm things that help each of you focus on Jesus. Discuss ways such focus on Christ helps us throw off sin instead of becoming weary and losing heart. Examples follow:

    a. Focusing on Jesus' victory over Satan's temptations helps us throw off the sin of coveting things God has not given us, instead of grabbing for them (Matthew 4:3–10) as we remember that Christ in us resists sin.

    b. Focusing on Jesus, who did not have a bed or pillow (Matthew 8:20), can help us throw off the sin of complaining over hardships in our lives, as we believe that Jesus in us can be content.

    c. Focusing on Jesus, who bore many insults (Matthew 11:19), can help us throw off the sin of feeling sorry for ourselves when people mistreat us. Joined with Jesus, we can also trust and honor God when people call us names.

Notes

Notes

9. Ask God to help the children throw off the sin that weighs them down and makes it hard for them to joyfully run the race God has laid out for them. Ask God to give the children grace to persevere.

Options:

You may time the children as they do activities with and without the weighted backpacks to demonstrate that it is better to race with less weight.

Review:

1. As opportunities arise, discuss ways that sin weighs you and your children down: paying attention to friends during worship, thinking about video games during school, reading books after being told to go to sleep, etc.

2. Pray, asking God to forgive those sins and help each of you run the race of the Christian life in ways that honor God.

Lesson 52

To Hear God's Gentle Whisper

Big Ideas

- *It is important to pay attention so we can hear God's quiet whisper as he speaks through the Bible (1 Kings 19:9–12; 2 Timothy 3:16).*
- *God works in us to help us want to obey him and to actually obey him (Philippians 2:13).*

ATTENDING TO VISUAL INFORMATION; WORKING SILENTLY; FOCUSING INTENTLY

Materials

- Bible
- Items for making sound effects, (hidden behind a screen) or sound effects CD/ website
- Download the two almost identical pictures of Elijah on Mount Carmel: Picture-30 and Picture-31, and print *both* for each child (see page 288)
- Optional: graph paper and pencil; timer

Activity:

1. Review the "Head, Shoulders, Hands to Toes" song, then have the children sit quietly while you explain that this activity focuses on paying attention with their hands and heads—their brains, ears, and mouths.

2. Pray, thanking God that he speaks through his Word and asking God to help the children listen to his Word.

3. Read 1 Kings 19:9–12. Make sure the children understand that Elijah did not hear God in the mighty wind, the powerful earthquake, or the raging fire. Imagine together how carefully Elijah must have been paying attention to hear God's gentle whisper.

4. Have the children pay attention with their ears as you make or play different sounds. Ask the children to identify them.

Notes

5. Have the children work silently and pay attention with their eyes by finding seven differences between the two similar illustrations of the account of Elijah at Mount Carmel (see Picture-30 and Picture-31 on page 288).

6. After the children have finished this silent activity, discuss differences between the two pictures. Have each child tell one difference, making sure not to repeat any answers given previously.

7. Remind the children that it is easier to pay attention and work silently during a game, but God can also work in them to help them want to obey him and actually obey as they worship, do schoolwork, and help with chores (Philippians 2:13).

8. Ask God to help the children want to pay attention to him. Thank God that he works in us to help us *want* to obey him and to actually obey him (Philippians 2:13).

Notes

Options:

1. These activities may be completed in two or more sittings. Steps 1–3 may be done in the first sitting. Step 4 may be done separately, after a quick review of 1 Kings 19:9–12. Steps 5–7 may be done in a third session.

2. If the children are beginning to work silently for longer periods of time, make a graph charting the children's increasing attention spans. This will glorify God's grace and power while encouraging the children's hope and motivation.

Review:

Notes

1. In order to catch the children practicing attentive behaviors, you will have to be attentive to God's quiet whisper as he rejoices over their small steps of faith and obedience.

2. Jesus knows how to sustain the weary with a word (Isaiah 50:4–5). Encourage your children so they will not grow weary of doing good, for God will reward them in due time (Galatians 6:9). Jesus awoke each day to hear God's voice and God opened Jesus' ear to both hear and obey (Isaiah 50:4–5). Children who are joined with Jesus by faith can listen to God as he speaks through Scripture, then obey his Word.

Lesson 53

To Please God

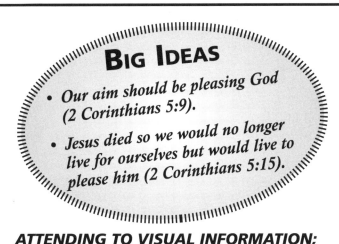

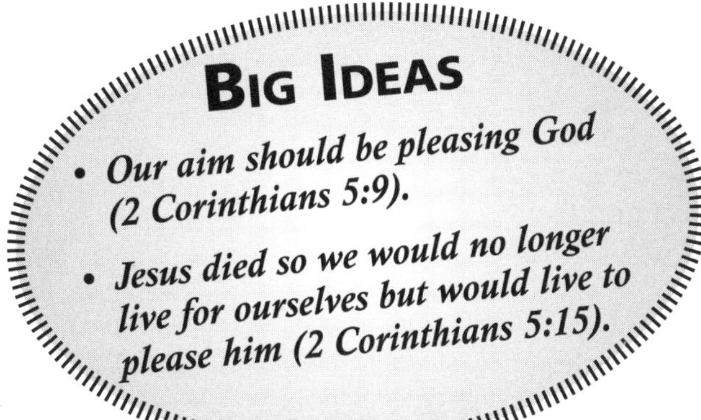

BIG IDEAS
• Our aim should be pleasing God (2 Corinthians 5:9).
• Jesus died so we would no longer live for ourselves but would live to please him (2 Corinthians 5:15).

ATTENDING TO VISUAL INFORMATION; WORKING SILENTLY; FOCUSING INTENTLY

Materials

- Bible
- Coffee stirrers
- Straws (large enough that coffee stirrers fit inside them)

Notes

Activity:

1. Review the "Head, Shoulders, Hands to Toes" song, then have the children sit quietly while you explain that this activity focuses on paying attention with their hands and heads—their brains and eyes.

2. Review ways to use the gift of their bodies to pay attention:

- Heads:
  Brain, eyes, and ears on task.
  Mouths closed or talking only on task.
  Shoulders and backs straight.
- Hands:
  Folded or moving only as instructed.
  Raised to get permission before speaking.
- Legs still.

3. Thank God for the way he has been helping the children learn to be attentive. Ask God to help them be attentive now. Thank God that Jesus died so that we could and would live for him (2 Corinthians 5:15).

4. Ask the children for reasons why it is important to pay attention when parents and teachers are talking. Read 2 Corinthians 5:9b: "… we make it our aim to please him"(ESV). Explain that paying attention to parents and teachers honors them and pleases God who commands us to honor those in authority over us.

5. Read 2 Corinthians 5:15. Explain that Jesus died so we would no longer live for ourselves but would live to please him. Brainstorm ways of pleasing God.

6. Hold a coffee stirrer in one hand and a straw in the other. With both arms fully extended out from your shoulders, carefully bring both arms in front of your body so that the smaller stirrer fits inside the larger straw.

7. Have the children try this straw activity ten times while reciting 2 Corinthians 5:9b.

8. Pray, asking God to help each of you aim even more carefully to please him in all things.

Notes

Options:

1. The activity in Steps 6–7 may be modified by having the children bend their arms so that the straw and stirrer are closer to their bodies, making it easier to fit the stirrer inside the straw.

2. This activity may also be modified to make it more difficult by having the children perfectly fit the stirrer inside the straw (without first hitting the rim of the straw).

Review:

Use the straw and stirrer often to review this verse and its gospel application that Jesus died so we would no longer live for ourselves but would live for him (2 Corinthians 5:15).

Lesson 54

To Live

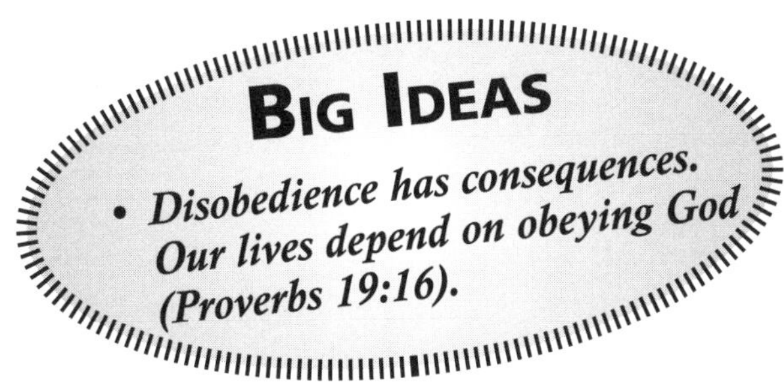
BIG IDEAS
• Disobedience has consequences. Our lives depend on obeying God (Proverbs 19:16).

LISTENING ATTENTIVELY

Materials

- Bible
- Optional: paper and pencils, crayons, and/or markers
- Timer

Notes

Activity:

1. Review the "Head, Shoulders, Hands to Toes" song, then have the children sit quietly while you explain that this activity focuses on paying attention with their heads—their brains, ears, and mouths.

2. Ask God to help the children please him by listening attentively to his quiet whisper in the Bible.

3. Read or retell either of the following accounts from Scripture:

   a. God blessing Noah's faith and obedience by saving the lives of his family: Genesis 6:11–22; 7:6–24.

   b. God blessing the Israelites' faith and obedience by saving the lives of their firstborn sons: Exodus 12:21–32.

4. Briefly discuss what would have happened if the people had not listened to and obeyed God.

5. Read Proverbs 19:16. Press home the point that our lives depend on obeying God.

6. Point out that Jesus always obeyed, but died to take the consequences of our disobedience. Because of what Jesus has done, God forgives

the disobedience of everyone who believes in him (1 Peter 2:24; Romans 8:3–4).

7. Pray together, asking God to forgive specific acts and attitudes of disobedience. Thank God for Jesus and the many blessings he gives to those who believe in him.

Notes

Options:

1. Having the children draw a picture of the Bible story as you read it may encourage their quiet and attentive listening.

2. This activity may be repeated using other accounts from Scripture. It may also be repeated using stories from your own life.

3. The shelves of home and public libraries are filled with stories that illustrate the consequences of disobedience. Challenge the children to find examples as they listen to children's literature. Encourage attentiveness to stories read aloud by beginning with short snippets of picture books. At first, you may need to celebrate the grace God gives the children to listen attentively to one or two pages of a picture book. Take as many sittings as necessary to finish that book, thanking God together each time he gives the children grace to attend to short sections of the book.

4. Gradually, lengthen the books (or portions of books) the children can listen to in one sitting or progress to more elaborate picture books that highlight the consequences of disobedience. Eventually, increase the length and complexity of the books until the children can listen to chapter books. Encourage the children by graphing the increasing amounts of time they succeed in listening attentively.

5. Help the children transfer their attention skills to other settings such as corporate and/or family worship.

Review:

As the children's attention spans develop, keep thanking God together for the grace and power he is giving them to become more attentive.

Notes

Lesson 55

To Honor

Big Ideas

- *We should receive the punishment our sins deserve, but Christ died for his people (Romans 3:21–26) and gives them his perfect record (Romans 8:3–4).*
- *Jesus always honored God (John 8:29). Christians are united with Christ (Romans 6), so they can honor God (1 Corinthians 6:20) and others (Romans 12:10).*

Materials

- Bible
- Picture-12 *Courtroom & Judge* on page 279
- Timer
- At least three participants

Notes

REMAINING ATTENTIVE IN THE MIDST OF TEMPTING DISTRACTIONS

Activity:

1. Review the "Head, Shoulders, Hands to Toes" song, then have the children sit quietly while you explain that this activity focuses on paying attention with their heads—their brains, eyes, and mouths—and with their whole bodies "head to toe."

2. Pray, asking God to help the children obey God by obeying you.

3. Introduce the concepts of judges and courtrooms.

   a. Show Picture-12 *Courtroom and Judge.*

   b. Explain that everyone in the courtroom must honor the judge.

   c. When the judge enters the courtroom, everyone is instructed to rise.

d. People in the courtroom must dress in ways that are respectful. Judges can have people removed for dressing in ways they find disrespectful.

e. People may not speak unless the judge has spoken to them.

f. People address the judge as "Your honor."

g. No one is allowed to interrupt the judge or argue with him or her.

4. Explain that, in court, someone who is accused of disobeying the law comes before the judge. People who know whether that person disobeyed the law may need to come to the court to testify. These people are called witnesses.

5. Review 1 Corinthians 6:20. Remind your child to honor God by sitting up straight—with hands folded, feet still, and eyes on you.

6. Read Romans 12:10. Explain that one way to honor God is to honor the people he has made in his image and the authorities he has put over us.

7. Have three or more participants act out a courtroom scene:

   a. The parent or teacher plays the part of the judge.

   b. One person plays the part of the accused person.

   c. One person plays the part of a witness.

   d. Additional participants will get turns later.

8. The accused person sits or stands in front of the judge. Remind the accused that honoring the judge can make a difference in whether that judge views him or her as guilty.

9. The witness sits or stands just behind the judge. While the accused is answering simple questions from the judge (name, age, address, etc.), the witness (who is positioned just out of the judge's sight line) makes faces and gestures—trying to distract the accused.

Notes

Notes

10. A different witness may be brought to try to get the accused to dishonor the judge.

11. Time how long the accused continues to honor the judge without laughing or looking away from the judge. Celebrate the accused person's self-control.

12. Repeat Steps 7–10 until all the children have had turns.

13. Read Isaiah 33:22. Explain that we are all accused and found guilty in God's courtroom. We should receive the terrible punishment our sins deserve. God, our judge, became our Savior. Jesus took our record of crimes and put his name on our bad records. If we believe in Jesus, he gives us his perfect record that has no sin and is full of the good things Jesus did to honor God every minute of his life (Romans 8:3–4; John 8:29). Christians are united with Christ so they can honor God and others (Romans 12:10).

14. Thank God that Jesus, who always honored God, forgives us for not honoring God and others. Pray for forgiveness and grace to honor God and others.

Options:

1. This game may also be played silently so children do not have to answer questions, but must not move or laugh while keeping their eyes locked upon the judge.

2. The children I have worked with never tire of this game. They become amazingly skilled at honoring the judge no matter how outrageous the antics of the witnesses become. Let the children explain the creative means they develop to discipline themselves to avoid laughing. Children also love trying out the role of judge.

Review:

When you confront the children with their sin, remind them that Jesus can save them from this sin. If they believe in Jesus, the Holy Spirit lives in them to honor God by paying attention to his still, small voice speaking through his Word. If they believe in Jesus, Jesus lives in them to honor other people by listening attentively to them.

Notes

Lesson 56

To Avoid Drifting Away

Big Ideas

- *God tells us to pay careful attention so we do not drift away from the gospel (Hebrews 2:1–3).*
- *The Holy Spirit helps us pay careful attention to the things Christ taught (John 14:23, 26).*

SELF-MONITORING

Materials

- Bible
- Toy car or train
- Inclined track (which can be made from books or boards)
- Material for engaging activity (see Step 5)
- Optional: paper and pencil; books

Notes

Activity:

1. Review the "Head, Shoulders, Hands to Toes" song, then have the children sit quietly while you explain that this activity focuses on paying attention with their hands and heads—their brains, eyes, and mouths.

2. Ask God to help the children honor him by honoring you with attentive listening.

3. Review ways to use the gift of their bodies to pay attention:

- Heads:
  Brain, eyes, and ears on task.
  Mouths closed or talking only on task.
- Shoulders and backs straight.
- Hands:
  Folded or moving only as instructed.
  Raised to get permission before speaking.
- Legs still.

4. Have the children make an inclined track. Tell one child to hold a toy car or train at the top of the track.

5. Do some engaging activity while that child holds the vehicle at the top of the track. (The point is to distract the child's attention so he or she lets go of the vehicle.) Read a book, offer a snack, or direct the child's attention to something outside.

6. If, after some time, the child has not let the vehicle fall down the incline, thank God for helping him or her to be so attentive. Ask what would have happened if the child's attention had drifted. Let the children demonstrate.

7. If your child allows the vehicle to slip down the incline, talk about how and why his or her attention wandered from the task of holding the car at the top of the hill.

8. Discuss situations in which serious consequences could occur as a result of not paying attention: wrecking cars, slamming fingers in doors, falling down stairs, getting cut with knives, etc.

9. Read Hebrews 2:1–3. Explain that not paying attention to what God says in the Bible can result in much worse consequences than wrecking cars, slamming fingers in doors, falling down stairs, or getting cut with knives. In Hebrews 2:3, God warns that he will punish anyone who drifts away from following his Word.

10. Explain that The Holy Spirit helps us pay careful attention to the gospel (John 14:23, 26). Paying attention to parents and teachers helps us practice for paying attention to God. The Holy Spirit also helps us obey God by paying attention to parents and teachers (John 14:15–16).

11. Pray, thanking God that the Holy Spirit helps us pay attention to God's Word, so we do not drift away from God.

Notes

Options:

Notes

1. Ask the children when and how often their attention drifts.

2. Ask if there are certain activities when they are especially prone to drifting. Teach them to monitor their attentiveness by putting tally marks on a piece of paper to indicate when they are thinking about what they are hearing.

3. This type of self-monitoring should be repeated often, especially during read-aloud books. Self-monitoring can be done in many settings to encourage children to transfer the skills they are developing in attentive listening. Give the children measurable feedback on their progress by commenting on how many tally marks they made for paying attention.

4. Read some of following verses, which warn of the consequences of moving away from God: Revelation 2:4–5 and 3:2–4; 2 Peter 2; Luke 9:62; Malachi 3:7; Ezekiel 18:24; John 15:6. Read 3 John 1:9 and discuss what Diotrephes was and was not paying attention to (paying attention to being first, rather than putting God first). Read 2 Timothy 4:10 and discuss what Demas was and was not paying attention to (the world, rather than God).

5. Some children may be instructed by hearing stories of the consequences of drifting. The Internet[25] abounds with examples that serve as warnings.

25 My quick Internet search found a newspaper article about a man who floated a mile into the Gulf of Mexico on a pool raft, a child who let a boat drift to a dangerous waterfall, and a Navy ship that lost anchor and began drifting toward a supply vessel.

Review:

Every sin involves drifting from God—and from the grace he can give us to obey. When the children disobey, bring their attention back to the gospel.

Notes

Lesson 57

To Be Strong in Grace

Big Ideas

- *Sometimes the consequences of not paying attention and following directions are minor (such as having to redo a worksheet). Other times, the consequences of not paying attention and following directions are matters of life and death (Genesis 3).*
- *Jesus endured hardship, and his grace makes us strong to endure like good soldiers who are focused on his commands (2 Timothy 2:1, 3–4).*
- *Jesus ran his race, and his grace makes us strong to run as he commands (2 Timothy 2:5; Psalm 119:32).*

Materials

- Bible
- Download Picture-32 *Follow Directions Worksheet* (see page 288) and print for each child
- Pencils

Notes

PAYING ATTENTION TO DIRECTIONS

Activity:

1. Review the "Head, Shoulders, Hands to Toes" song, then have the children sit quietly while you explain that this activity focuses on paying attention with their heads—their brains and ears—and their entire bodies "head-to-toe."

2. Ask God to give the children grace to live self-controlled and holy lives (Titus 2:11–12).

3. If the children can read, give them Picture-32 *Follow Directions Worksheet* (see page 288). Tell them to complete them.

4. If the children cannot read, give them Picture-32 *Follow Directions Worksheet* (see page 288) and read the entire worksheet to them before allowing them to begin doing it. Surprisingly, even children who listen to the directions generally do not follow them on this tricky worksheet.

5. Score the children's worksheets right away. If the children followed the directions, thank God for the grace he gave them to pay attention to the right things. If the children did not follow the directions, ask what they were paying attention to (other than the directions). Explain that sometimes the consequences of not paying attention and following directions are minor (such as having to redo a worksheet). Sometimes, however, the consequences are very serious.

6. Read Genesis 3:1–19. Discuss the consequences of Adam and Eve not paying attention and following directions.

7. Read 2 Timothy 2:1, 3–4. Explain that Jesus endured the hardship of the cross like a good soldier who wanted to please God as his commanding officer.

8. Ask what soldiers have to pay attention to and whom soldiers have to obey. Discuss things that could happen if soldiers paid attention to the wrong things (if the soldiers were playing cards, looking at birds in the jungle, or reading books, for example) when enemy soldiers attacked. Discuss things that could happen if soldiers were trying to please the wrong people (the enemy, relatives back home, etc.) instead of aiming to please the commanding officer.

9. Explain that those who believe in Jesus are soldiers in God's army. God is their commanding officer. Jesus makes them strong by his grace, so they endure like good soldiers who are focused on his commands (2 Timothy 2:1, 3–4).

10. Discuss things that could go wrong when we pay attention to the wrong things (instead of paying

NOTES

attention to God, parents, and teachers) or try to please someone other than God.

Notes

11. Read 2 Timothy 2:5. Discuss ways athletes can be disqualified for not competing according to the rules:
    a. Swimmers who miss the wall on flip turns are disqualified.
    b. Runners who step outside their lanes are disqualified.
    c. Runners who make two false starts are disqualified.
12. Jesus ran his race, and his grace makes us strong to run the way of his commands (2 Timothy 2:5; Psalm 119:32).
13. Thank God that Jesus endured the hardship of the cross like a good soldier who wanted to please God as his commanding officer. Thank God that Jesus ran his race well without being disqualified. Thank God that, when we believe in Jesus, Jesus in us can endure hardship, please God, and run the race God has marked out for us.

Options:

1. Supplement this activity with physical races that have plenty of rules the children must follow to avoid disqualification.
2. Scripture mentions people who were disqualified in the Christian race. Discuss the examples and warnings given in 1 John 2:19 and 3 John 1:9.

Review:

Every time the children sin, they are paying attention to the wrong thing and refusing to endure hardship like a good soldier who wants to please God. Thank God that Jesus never wavered in his attention to God and never yielded to the temptation to make his life easier through disobedience (Matthew 4:1–10). Encourage the children to believe in this strong soldier. Then remind them that Jesus in them can pay attention to the right things, please God, endure hardship, and race to the glory of God.

Notes

Lesson 58

To Be Blessed

Big Ideas
• Those who obey God are under his blessing (John 13:17; Luke 11:28; James 1:25).

Materials

- Bible

Notes

LISTENING & REMEMBERING; TRANSITIONING BETWEEN MOVEMENT AND STILLNESS

Activity:

1. Review the "Head, Shoulders, Hands to Toes" song, then have the children sit quietly. while you explain that this activity focuses on paying attention with their hands and heads—their brains, eyes, ears, and mouths.

2. Ask God to bless the children as they obey him.

3. Ask the children to listen carefully to the following verses to find what good thing happens for those who obey: John 13:17; Luke 11:28; James 1:25 (being blessed by God).

4. Explain that being under God's blessing does not mean the children will be rich or healthy, pass all their tests in school, or win their soccer games. Being under God's blessing is being under his smile and having his, "Well done," as the banner over their lives.

5. Make the gospel clear by explaining that Jesus, who always obeyed, was under God's curse on the cross (Galatians 3:10–13), so that everyone who believes in Jesus can be under God's blessing.

Notes

6. Read and discuss Ephesians 6:1–3. Explain that children who obey their parents are under God's blessing.

7. Reinforce the connection between obedience and blessing, by playing "Mother (or Father, or Teacher), may I?"

   a. The parent/teacher stands at one end of a room, hallway, driveway, or yard.

   b. The children stand at the other end by some kind of landmark or marker indicating the starting line.

   c. The parent/teacher gives a particular child a set of directions:

   d. "You may take two baby steps."

   e. "You may take one banana-split step."

   f. "You may take three bunny hops."

   g. "You may take one kangaroo leap."

   h. "You may take four ballerina twirls."

8. Before the child follows the directions, he or she must ask, "Mother (or Father, or Teacher), may I?"

9. If, at any point in the game, the child forgets to ask, "Mother, may I?" that child must return to the starting line.

10. Play continues until someone reaches the leader and becomes the new leader.

11. Pray, thanking God that Jesus always obeyed but was cursed when he took the punishment for our disobedience (Galatians 3:10–13). Thank God that we are blessed because of Jesus' obedience (Galatians 3:14). Ask God to help the children obey.

Options:

1. The game in Step 7 may be varied in the following way to increase the demand for attentiveness. If the child remembers to ask, "Mother, may I?" the leader may do either of the following:

- Grant permission, so the child takes the appointed number and type of steps.
- Deny permission and give a new instruction, in which case the child must remember to ask again, "Mother, may I?" (returning to the starting line if this step is overlooked).

Notes

Review:

1. As you read the Bible with the children, point out instances of people being blessed as they obeyed. Examples follow:

   Luke 17:11–14. Would the ten people have been healed of leprosy if they had not moved to obey?

   2 Kings 5:1–14. Would Namaan have been healed if he had not obeyed?

2. When the children sin, point them to Christ's perfect record of obedience and encourage them that, when they believe in Jesus, his perfect record is theirs.

Lesson 59

To Be a Vessel of Honor

Big Ideas

- *If I dishonor God and others, I am a dishonorable vessel (2 Timothy 2:20–21).*
- *If I cleanse myself from what is dishonorable, I can be an honorable vessel for God's glory (2 Timothy 2:21).*
- *The blood of Christ cleanses us from sin (1 John 1:7), so we can be honorable vessels.*

WORKING SILENTLY; ATTENDING TO VISUAL DETAIL

Materials

- Bible
- Optional:
- Download and print for each child:
  Picture-33 *Vessel of Honor*,
  Picture-34 *Boy with Vessel*
- Download Picture-35 *Completed Vessel* and print one for teacher reference (see page 288)
- Stiff blank paper
- Colored pencils, scissors, paper, glue or rubber cement

Notes

Activity:

1. Review the "Head, Shoulders, Hands to Toes" song, then have the children sit quietly.
2. Ask God to bless the children in their efforts to obey.
3. Tell the children that they will have to listen very carefully to the following verses to find what good thing happens for those who obey:
   a. John 12:26b (honor).
   b. Matthew 5:19 (being called great).
4. Imagine a scenario in which the children might be honored by someone important:
   a. A television crew featuring them because of the great work they did in school.

Notes

   b. A sports hero coming to see them play and praising them for a job well done.

   c. The president inviting them to the White House to congratulate them for making peace with siblings or classmates.

5. Discuss the greater honor of being honored by the king of the universe.

6. Read 2 Timothy 2:20–21. Contrast the different uses of honorable and dishonorable vessels: the beautiful, honorable vessels were used for serving food and drink; the dishonorable vessels were ancient toilets.

7. Explain that, if we dishonor God and others, we are dishonorable vessels (2 Timothy 2:20–21). If we cleanse ourselves from what is dishonorable, we can be honorable vessels for God's glory (2 Timothy 2:21).

8. Discuss sins each of you needs to cleanse yourselves from in order to be beautiful, honorable vessels that are useful to God.

9. Read 1 John 1:7. Brainstorm ways to live out the truth that we are cleansed from sin:

   a. Would children who are cleansed from sin treasure a toy so much that they have tantrums when it's time to stop playing?

   b. Would children who are cleansed from sin love winning so much that they would cheat at games?

10. Thank God that Jesus took on the dishonor of our sin and clothes us in the honor of his glory. Ask God to help the children cleanse themselves from what is dishonorable so they can be honorable vessels for God's glory. Thank God for his power to help us live as honorable vessels who are cleansed from sin.

Options:

Use the following directions to make a reversible picture from Picture-33 *Vessel of Honor* and Picture-34 *Boy with Vessel* (see page 288).

1. Color each picture with colored pencils, using very different colors on the two pictures. For example, if you use orange, green, and yellow on the vase, you might use blue, brown, and purple for the child on the chamber pot. It is important to use colored pencils (rather than markers or crayons), so the pre-marked vertical lines printed on each picture will still show.

2. Cut a piece of stiff paper, 8.5 x 11 inches. Turn it horizontally, so that it is 8.5 inches in height (like the picture the children just colored) and 11 inches wide.

3. Cut each colored picture into strips along the pre-marked vertical lines, making sure not to cut off the letter-number marks (1A, 1B, etc.) at the bottom of each strip.

4. Glue the colored and cut-apart strips to the blank paper, starting at the left-hand side with strip 1A. Glue strip 2A to the right of 1A. Glue 1B next, then glue 2B, etc. Leave a small margin between the strips (to allow room for accordion folding in Step 5). See Picture-35 *Completed Vessel* on page 288.

5. After the glue dries, accordion fold the paper along the the margins between each strip. Fold so the picture strips are still visible and 1A and 2A form a mountain, 1B and 2B form a mountain, etc. When you view the completed picture from the side, you should see a child ingloriously seated on a chamber pot. When you view the picture from the other side, you should see a beautiful vase.

6. Use this picture to encourage the children that, as they rely on God's power and grace, they can be vessels "for honorable use, set apart as holy, useful to the master…, ready for every good work" (2 Timothy 2:21 ESV).

Notes

Review:

Notes

1. When the children sin, help them confess their dishonorable actions and attitudes.

2. Ask God to help them put on honorable actions and attitudes to make them beautiful for use in God's house.

Lesson 60

To Build on the Rock

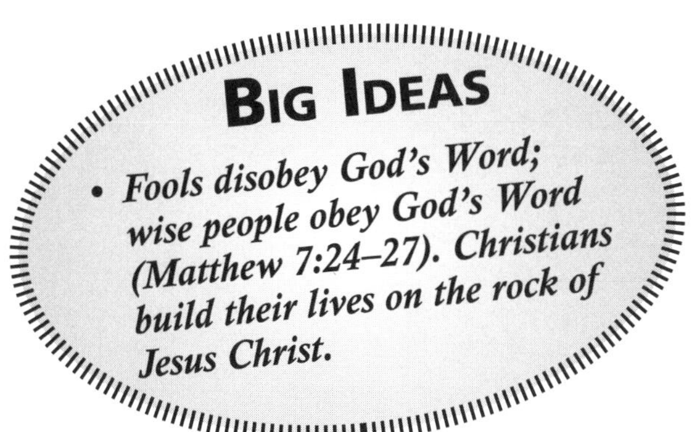

Big Ideas
• Fools disobey God's Word; wise people obey God's Word (Matthew 7:24–27). Christians build their lives on the rock of Jesus Christ.

Materials

- Bible
- Blocks
- Download Picture-36 *Pitfall Maze* (see page 288) and print for each child
- Crayons, markers, and/or pencils

ATTENDING TO VISUAL DETAIL

Activity:

1. Review the "Head, Shoulders, Hands to Toes" song, then have the children sit quietly while you explain that this activity focuses on paying attention with their hands and heads—their brains, ears, and mouths.

2. Pray that God would help the children learn the wisdom of obedience.

3. Ask the children to listen carefully to a story Jesus told, so they can learn what happens to people who wisely obey God and people who foolishly disobey.

4. Read Matthew 7:24–27. Have the children act out the story by using the blocks to build a strong house with a good foundation and a house with a rickety foundation. Crash the house built on the rickety foundation.

5. Read the following verses and discuss ways people build on a foolish foundation of disobedience to God's Word instead of on the strong foundation of obeying God:

Notes

Notes

a. Proverbs 10:8 (talking foolishly).

b. Proverbs 26:11 (returning to sinful attitudes or actions).

c. Proverbs 29:11 (blowing up in anger).

6. Have children complete Picture-36 *Pitfall Maze* (see page 288) by tracking with their eyes, being sure to avoid the foolish pitfalls.

7. After completing the maze with their eyes, the children may complete it with crayons, pencils, or markers.

8. Explain that Jesus, who was wise, took the punishment for our foolish disobedience, and gives his wisdom to those who believe in him (1 Corinthians 1:30).

9. Thank God that Jesus always chose the wise path of obedience and that he has become our wisdom and holiness (1 Corinthians 1:30). Ask God to build the children's lives on the rock of Jesus Christ.

Options:

1. This lesson may be supplemented with other examples of people who built on foolish foundations by disobeying God's Word:

- Moses' costly disobedience in Numbers 20:1–12.
- Achan's ruinous disobedience in Joshua 7:1–26.
- Saul's disastrous disobedience in 1 Samuel 15:1–26.
- The deadly rebellion of Korah, Dathan, and Abiram in Numbers 16:1–33.

2. Contrast these examples with Jesus' costly obedience on the cross.

Review:

1. Every time the children sin, they are building on a foundation other than Jesus Christ. Ask questions to help them see what foundation they are building on (inordinate desires, friendships, autonomy, etc.). Ask God to show them the foolishness of those foundations.

2. Ask God to work in them a deep desire to build their lives on Jesus Christ.

Notes

Lesson 61

For Eternal Benefit

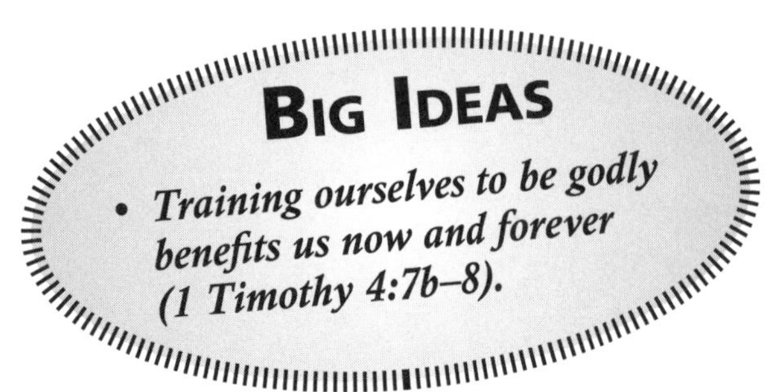
BIG IDEAS
• Training ourselves to be godly benefits us now and forever (1 Timothy 4:7b–8).

MATERIALS

- Bible
- Optional: leader may use a hole punch and rubber band to attach a "cheat sheet" to one hand

LISTENING; TRANSITIONING FROM ACTIVE MOVEMENT TO SILENT STILLNESS

NOTES

ACTIVITY:

1. Review the "Head, Shoulders, Hands to Toes" song, then have the children sit quietly.

2. Ask God to use his Word to equip the children for every good work (2 Timothy 3:16).

3. Read 1 Timothy 4:7b–8. Brainstorm some of the benefits of physical training (strength, coordination, energy, health, etc.). Explain that training our bodies to be strong can only benefit us in this world, but training ourselves to be like God benefits us now and forever.

4. Help the children train themselves to listen to and follow directions by playing this game:

   a. The leader demonstrates four clapping patterns and what action should be done with each specific clapping pattern:

   b. One clap might indicate that the children should stand up.

   c. Two claps might indicate that the children should march in place.

   d. Three claps done in quick succession might indicate that the children should turn around.

Notes

e. Three claps done in the rhythm of "Clap, clap ... pause ... clap," might indicate that the children should sit down.

5. The leader claps the various patterns while the children do the actions indicated. (The leader may jot down the clapping patterns on a "cheat sheet" to reference during the game.)

6. Reread 1 Timothy 4:7b–8. Explain that God is so gracious he gives us the desire to train ourselves in godliness (Philippians 2:13a) and the power to train ourselves in godliness (Philippians 2:13b). That training benefits us now and forever (1 Timothy 4:7b–8). Brainstorm ways each of you can train yourselves in godliness. Make specific plans to carry out those ideas.

7. Ask God to help the children train themselves in godliness so they will enjoy eternal benefits.

Options:

1. The game described in Step 4 may be adapted to make it more difficult and increase the demand for careful attention:
   a. Increase the number of clapping patterns.
   b. Increase the complexity of clapping patterns.
   c. Increase the complexity of actions that accompany the clapping patterns.
2. Allowing children to take turns leading the game will also develop the children's habits of paying attention.

Review:

Sometimes parents and teachers know beforehand that certain events and activities will be difficult for particular children. Prayerfully help those children prepare by reminding them that this opportunity to train themselves in godliness can benefit them forever.

Lesson 62

For a Good Harvest

Big Ideas

- *We reap what we sow. Sowing to please the flesh reaps destruction; sowing to please the Spirit reaps eternal life (Galatians 6:7–9).*
- *Jesus always obeyed God (John 14:31) and sowed to please the Spirit (John 8:28–29). As we believe in him, we reap eternal life that begins in joyful obedience here and now (John 3:36).*

Materials

- Bible
- Picture-13 *Acorn* on page 281
- Picture-14 *Cherries* on page 283
- Download Picture-37 *Tree* (see page 288) and print for each child
- Timer
- Objects that are small enough to fit in the children's hands
- Planter
- Something to completely cover the top of the planter
- Paper & pencils
- Clear cups
- Materials to make "dirt cups"
- Chocolate cookie or graham cracker crumbs
- Chocolate pudding or yogurt
- Candy seeds or nuts
- Spoons

ATTENDING TO TACTILE INFORMATION

Activity:

1. Review the "Head, Shoulders, Hands to Toes" song, then have the children sit quietly.
2. Ask God to help the children train themselves in godliness.
3. Show the children Picture-13 *Acorn* on page 281. Ask what will grow when the acorn is planted. Show the children Picture-14 *Cherries* on page 283. Ask what will grow when that seed is planted.
4. Read Galatians 6:7–9. Ask the children what they will get if they plant seeds of sin (trouble now and forever).

5. Tell the children to listen carefully for what will grow if they continue to plant seeds of paying attention, following directions, and obeying God. Read the following passages:

   a. Matthew 25:21 (joy).

   b. Ephesians 6:1–3 (life going well).

   c. John 12:26 (honor).

   d. Luke 11:28 (blessing).

   e. Isaiah 26:3 (peace).

   f. John 14:23 (God's loving presence).

   g. John 15:10 (abiding in God's love).

6. Emphasize that, if the children continue planting seeds of paying attention to and obeying God, they will reap a wonderful harvest forever.

7. Give each child a copy of Picture-37 *Tree* (see page 288), and help them fill in some of the bountiful harvest that grows from obedience.

8. Seat the children side-by-side on the floor. Have them put their hands behind their backs. Tell the children to play the following game silently. Time how long they can play silently.

   a. The leader passes an object to the first child, who feels it without looking at, then passes it to the next child.

   b. When the last child has felt the object, the leader drops it in a large planter that is situated behind the children (making sure the children do not see it).

   c. Meanwhile, as soon as the first child has finished feeling the first object, the leader gives that child a second object, which is also passed down the row, then dropped in the planter.

   d. Continue until ten objects have been passed down the row and dropped in the planter.

NOTES

Notes

   e. Keeping the planter covered, have the children write or draw all the objects they can remember.

   f. Let children tell one thing that they have listed. They must listen carefully as other children speak so they will not repeat previous answers. Praise them for planting so many seeds of paying attention as you pull the "seed" items from the planter.

9. Read Revelation 22:14. Celebrate God's grace in giving us access to the tree of life and helping the children increase their ability to sit still, keep quiet, and pay attention by making and enjoying "dirt cups" filled with the "seeds" of paying attention.

   a. Put the desired amount of "dirt" (chocolate or graham cracker crumbs) into each cup.

   b. Make the "dirt" muddy with either chocolate pudding or yogurt.

   c. Add "seeds" of candy and/or nuts.

10. Thank God that Jesus never wearied of doing good and ask God to help the children continue planting seeds of obedience by paying attention, following God's way, and doing new things that new people can do by faith.

Options:

For younger children, use fewer items for the game outlined in Step 8. To further develop the children's ability to pay attention, this game may be repeated with more (and/or more difficult) items. Graph how long the children attend silently and praise God for improved attentiveness.

Review:

Catch the children sowing seeds of attentiveness and cheer for them as they grow. Every time the children sin, help them discern what they were paying attention to (other than God).

LESSON 63

By Grace

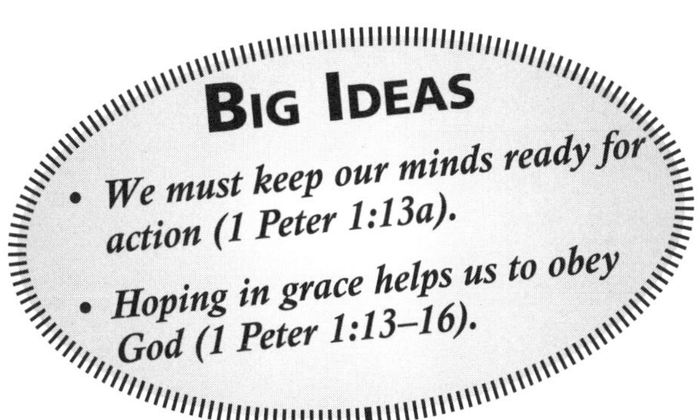

BIG IDEAS
• We must keep our minds ready for action (1 Peter 1:13a).
• Hoping in grace helps us to obey God (1 Peter 1:13–16).

MATERIALS

- Bible

NOTES

PRACTICING MENTAL ALERTNESS AND SELF-CONTROL

ACTIVITY:

1. Review the "Head, Shoulders, Hands to Toes" song, then have the children sit quietly.

2. Ask God to quiet the children's hearts and give them grace to follow the path of obeying God's Word that leads to eternal joy (Psalm 16:11).

3. Read 1 Peter 1:13a. Play the following game to help the children understand what it means to prepare their minds for actions God gives them grace to perform.

    a. Tell the children to move until you tell them to freeze.

    b. When the children freeze, they should remain still while preparing their minds for action by imagining something people in their positions might be preparing to do.

    c. Children must be self-controlled to remain frozen in their positions until the leader calls on them. When called on, the child says, "God has given me grace to…" completing the sentence with whatever he or she imagined, then briefly acting it out. For example, a child might imagine that he is in the position of a bowler about to release the bowling ball. That child would say, "God has given me grace to bowl," and throw the imaginary ball down the imaginary lane. Another child might imagine that she is in the position of an archer. She might say, "God has given me grace to shoot arrows," and release an imaginary arrow.

4. Discuss ways of preparing your body for action. Have the children demonstrate ways they prepare their bodies to do actions such as:
   a. Kicking a soccer ball.
   b. Doing ballet.
   c. Hitting a baseball.
   d. Jumping high.
5. Discuss ways of preparing your mind for action. Have the children explain what they might be thinking when their bodies are prepared to do any of the actions listed above.
6. Discuss ways the mind and body prepare to sin by pantomiming the body's stance and describing the mind's thoughts in instances such as the following:
   a. Getting ready to blow up when angry.
   b. Getting ready to pout when they do not get what they want.
7. Help the children understand that they do prepare their bodies and minds to sin. Explain that, when we sin, we are forgetting the grace that empowers holiness.
8. Read 1 Peter 1:13–16. Explain that hoping in grace helps us to obey God. Brainstorm ways the children can prepare their bodies and train their minds to be holy by thinking about God's powerful grace. Discuss the following scenarios or develop scenarios that fit the children's lives:
   a. Getting ready to blow up when angry so that their bodies are tense and their minds are filled

Notes

Notes

with angry thoughts, then praying for grace, relaxing their shoulders, taking a deep breath, and thanking God for the peace and joy of the Holy Spirit.

b. Getting ready to pout—with their minds full of demands for what they want—then praying for grace, remembering that Jesus always wanted what God wanted, giving their desires to God, and trusting God with unmet longings.

9. Pray, asking God to help the children prepare their minds for action, be self-controlled, set their hope on the grace of Jesus, and live holy lives.

Options:

The game explained in Step 3 may be varied if the adult says, "God has given you grace to…" The child silently pantomimes the scenario she has imagined. When called on, other children guess what the child was pantomiming by saying, "God has given you grace to fly an airplane?" or "God has given you grace to wash an elephant?"

Review:

Every time we sin we are forgetting the grace that empowers holiness and is always available to us. Lead the children in confessing the sin of forgetting God's grace. As you see them being tempted to sin, lovingly plead with them to remember God's grace and act in accordance with that grace.

LESSON 64

By Unpacking the Gospel Suitcase

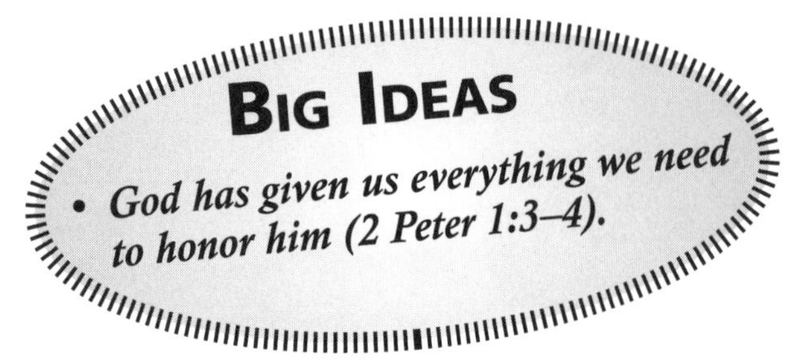

BIG IDEAS
• God has given us everything we need to honor him (2 Peter 1:3–4).

PRACTICING VISUAL AND AUDITORY ATTENTION

MATERIALS

- Bible
- Small suitcase
- Objects that fit inside that suitcase
- Pictures of things that are powerful (cut from magazines or printed from the Internet)
- Optional: Other items and/or pictures

NOTES

ACTIVITY:

1. Pray, thanking God for giving us everything we need to obey him.

2. Tell the children to remain silent while you show them the suitcase filled with objects. Do not explain that the children are to remember the objects; this allows the leader and the children to see whether the children are developing habits of attentiveness without specific prompting. Allow the children to look at the objects for one minute, or until someone makes noise, then close the suitcase.

3. Have the children work silently writing the names, or drawing pictures, of the objects.

4. Invite the children to take turns telling you the objects they saw. Instruct them to listen very carefully so they do not repeat a previous answer.

5. If the children cannot remember all the objects, repeat the game.

6. After the children have named all the objects, ask what strategies they used to remember the items.

7. Choose a specific location that is very different from the place where you live. For example, if it

is currently hot where you live, pick Alaska. If you are in the midst of winter, choose Hawaii or Puerto Rico. Ask the children what they would pack if you were taking them there.

8. Have the children imagine they are traveling to that place with everything they need in their suitcases. If imagining travel to Alaska, the suitcase might have snowsuits for outdoor play, snowshoes for trekking to see animals, etc. If imagining travel to Puerto Rico, the suitcase might have bathing suits for playing at the beach and snorkels for seeing beautiful tropical fish. If the children do not open their suitcases, they will be miserably cold in Alaska and miserably hot in Puerto Rico.

9. Read 2 Peter 1:3–4. Explain that God has so much power that he has given us everything we need to pay attention to God and follow his Word. Think of this as a gospel suitcase filled with everything we need to overcome sin and become like Jesus. God joins believers with Jesus so they can obey (Galatians 2:20). He gives us a helper, who helps us obey—the Holy Spirit (John 14:16). We open this gospel suitcase by reading the Bible so we can know God. We open this gospel suitcase by praying for grace to obey. Encourage the children to open the gospel suitcase when they are tempted to drift, pay attention to the wrong things, or disobey.

10. Teach the children about the divine power referenced in 2 Peter 1:3 by packing the suitcase with pictures that show powerful things (tornadoes, fires, lightning, weight lifters, volcanoes, kings, exploding stars, etc.). Play the memory game (from Steps 2–6) again using these pictures.

11. Afterward, ask if any of the children can figure out what the items have in common (things that are strong, or things that have power). Explain that the greatest power in the universe is not in hurricanes or tsunamis. The greatest power is in God (Job 26:12–14; Psalm 62:11; Jeremiah 10:12;

Notes

Romans 1:20), and his power has given us everything we need for life and godliness, so that we can resist temptation and become like him.

12. Pray, thanking God that his power has given us everything we need for life and godliness.

Options:

1. The memory game may be repeated with different objects or pictures in the suitcase. If the objects are selected according to a common theme, children can learn how helpful it is to organize things they want to remember around a theme. For children who can read, this activity may be repeated with written words, then made more difficult by using more advanced words.

2. This activity may also be done like the "I went to the store and bought..." game, using a suitcase theme to remind children that God has given us a gospel suitcase:

   a. The first participant would say, "My suitcase is packed with ...[item beginning with the letter **a**]," then slide the suitcase to the next player.

   b. The second participant would say, "My suitcase is packed with [the item beginning with the letter **a**], and ..." [then add item beginning with the letter **b**]. That person would slide the suitcase to the next player, until players have gone through the entire alphabet.

3. You may increase the demand for focus by using the following variations:

   a. Have players name any object, regardless of alphabetical order.

   b. Pass the suitcase to any player (making it harder to remember who said what, and making each child remain constantly attentive).

Notes

Review:

When you yield to discouragement, you have forgotten to unpack your gospel suitcase. Cry out to God with your children, asking God to help all of you unpack the suitcase that always has everything you need.

Notes

Lesson 65

By Putting Off, Renewing Thoughts, and Putting On

Big Ideas

- *God's grace and power enable Christians to put off the old self with its desire to pay attention to the wrong things (Ephesians 4:22).*
- *God's grace and power enable Christians to think in new ways (Ephesians 4:23) by remembering that they are joined with Jesus (Romans 6) who always paid attention to God.*
- *God's grace and power enable Christians to put on the new self which pays attention to God, parents, teachers, and other authorities (Ephesians 4:24).*

Materials

- Bible
- Old, stained clothing that is large enough to wear over the children's clothing, but small enough that the children will not trip over it
- Clothing that is special to the children: shimmering blouses, knight's armor, etc. – these articles must be large enough to wear over the children's clothing, but small enough that the children will not trip over them
- Optional: video recording device

Notes

THINKING NEW THOUGHTS

Activity:

1. Review the "Head, Shoulders, Hands to Toes" song, then have the children sit quietly while you explain that this activity focuses on paying attention with their hands and heads—their brains, ears, and mouths.

2. Pray, thanking God for the gospel suitcase he has given us.

NOTES

3. Review ways to use the gift of their bodies to pay attention:
   - Heads:
     Brain, eyes, and ears on task.
     Mouths closed or talking only on task.
   - Shoulders and backs straight.
   - Hands:
     Folded or moving only as instructed.
     Raised to get permission before speaking.
   - Legs still.

4. Read Ephesians 4:22–24. Help the children understand the three things this passage tells them to do: put off the old, think new thoughts, and put on the new.

5. Help the children confess some of the old ways they need to put off, such as: drifting when they are supposed to be listening; paying attention to friends when they are supposed to be listening to the teacher; keeping the television on when they have been told to turn it off; saying hateful words; becoming angry when they don't get what they want; etc.

6. Help the children brainstorm new ways of thinking, such as: Jesus in me can pay attention (Isaiah 50:4b); God has given me power to listen to my teacher (2 Peter 1:3–5); Jesus always obeyed God and can help me obey (John 8:28–29); I have the Holy Spirit to help me obey (John 14:16–17); etc.

7. Help the children brainstorm new actions to put on: making themselves sit up straight when they catch themselves drifting; looking away from friends to focus on the teacher; obeying immediately when told to turn off the television; saying loving words; telling their parents that it would be their pleasure to obey.

8. One at a time, have children put the old clothes over their regular clothing and say what old, sinful

habit the old clothes represent ("Disobeying my parent or teacher," for example).

9. Have children throw off the old clothes and shout, ("With God's help, I can put off…" (disobedience for example). Have them shout a renewed thought (such as, "Jesus always obeyed God, so Jesus in me can obey," for example). Provide coaching as necessary.

10. Then let the children put on the new clothes, saying some new action or attitude these clothes represent, for example, "With God's help, I can obey my parent or teacher."

11. Repeat Steps 8–10 until every child has enjoyed a turn.

12. Pray, thanking God that he gives us power to put off stinky old sin, think new thoughts, and put on shiny new actions and attitudes.

Options:

If you have access to a video recording device, record this activity. Watching it together later provides an enjoyable and effective review.

Review:

Every time the children sin, encourage them to put off that stinky old habit. Model for them the renewed thoughts they can think. Cheer them on as they put on new actions and attitudes.

Notes

Lesson 66

By Sowing and Reaping

Big Ideas

- *We reap the fruit of the seeds we sow. Planting seeds of sin grows trouble and destruction. Planting seeds that please God's Spirit grows eternal life (Galatians 6:7–8).*
- *Jesus always sowed seeds that pleased God's Spirit, but took the punishment we deserve for planting seeds of sin. Joined with Christ, we can sow seeds to please God (Galatians 2:20).*

Materials

- Bible
- Train set or toy cars and a roadway made of blocks or books
- Objects that can be used as obstacles

Notes

WAITING SILENTLY

Activity:

1. Review the "Head, Shoulders, Hands to Toes" song, then have the children sit quietly.
2. Pray, thanking God for his great power that helps us to put off sin, think in new ways, and put on the actions and attitudes of Jesus.
3. Let the children make a **Y** track (like the one described in Section 2, Lessons 36 & 37).
4. Put obstacles along the right side of the track (hills, etc.).
5. Put insurmountable obstacles at the end of the left side of the track (roadblocks, broken track, etc.).
6. Read Galatians 6:7–8. Explain that we reap the fruit of the seeds we sow. Planting seeds

of sin grows trouble and destruction. Planting seeds that please God's Spirit grows eternal life (Galatians 6:7–8).[26]

7. Explain that the right side of the track represents sowing to please the Spirit by obeying God's Word. Explain that the left side of the track represents sowing to please the flesh.

8. On the right track, use the vehicles to show the children that the decision to please the Spirit and obey God's Word may be very difficult. Tell them the obstacles represent such difficulties, and give examples from their daily lives. There may be many hardships along the path of obedience.

9. Read Galatians 6:7–8 again. On the left track, use the vehicles to show the children that the decision to please the flesh may not seem to have problems at first, but always ends up being a dead end, because the one who sows to please his sinful nature will reap destruction.

10. Read Galatians 6:7–8 again. Ask the children what is at the end of the right track (eternal life).

11. Have the children take turns crashing the vehicles along the left side of the track and pushing the vehicles along the right path of eternal joy.

12. Pray, asking God to help the children make decisions that may feel very difficult but lead to life now and forever.

NOTES

26 I first saw this verse paired with a **Y** chart at an Association of Certified Biblical Counselors Counseling and Discipleship Training conference.

Options:

Notes

1. Repeat this activity, talking about the engine that drives the vehicle to follow either the right or the left path. The Bible refers to this engine as the heart.

2. Read and discuss Proverbs 4:23. As the children make decisions (either wisely or foolishly), ask questions that help the children see what motivations of the heart drove their words, decisions, and actions.

Review:

Every time the children sin, help them explore the feelings, thoughts, desires, and treasures that are the engines driving their lives along one path or another. When you sin, model this for them by repenting of heart attitudes (not just repenting of surface sinful behaviors).

Lesson 67

Celebrating with Jesus

Big Ideas

- *God created people to enjoy being attentive to him (Psalm 37:4) and following his direction (Psalm 16:11), but Adam and Eve paid attention to the wrong things and disobeyed God's direction (Genesis 3).*
- *Ever since Adam and Eve sinned, all people are born paying attention to the wrong things and disobeying God (Romans 1:18–23).*
- *Jesus always delighted in being attentive to God and following God's direction (John 8:28–29). Jesus died to take the punishment we deserve for paying attention to the wrong things and not following God's direction (Isaiah 53:6).*
- *People who believe in Jesus are made new. New people do new things, like paying attention to God and obeying him (1 Peter 2:24).*
- *Christians celebrate with Jesus now and forever (Revelation 3:20, 19:6–9).*

Materials

- Bible
- Tree or branch
- Treats (candy, dried fruit, etc.) in see-through bags
- Paper clips
- *Advance preparation: Prior to this lesson, use paper clips to attach the bags to some kind of tree. You may use a tree outside, "plant" a branch in a bucket of sand, etc.

REMAINING ATTENTIVE IN THE MIDST OF DISTRACTION AND TEMPTATION

Activity:

Notes

1. Have the children sit around the tree. Emphasize that all talk must be on task.

2. Pray, thanking God that Jesus always delighted in being attentive to God and following his direction. Ask God to help the children delight in being attentive to God.

3. As you read Genesis 1–3 or portions of those chapters (Genesis 2:4–10, 15–18, 21–23; 3:1–6), do not allow any discussion of the tree.

4. Discuss the following points, which outline a biblical perspective on attentiveness and obedience:

   a. **Creation:**

      God made Adam and Eve to pay attention to him and follow his directions.

      In the Garden of Eden, Adam and Eve could enjoy a banquet of delicious food. There was only one food they were not to eat.

   b. **Fall:**

      Adam and Eve paid attention to the serpent and the forbidden tree, instead of paying attention to God.

      Adam and Eve followed the serpent instead of following God's directions.

      Adam and Eve were shut out from that great banquet in the Garden.

      Ever since Adam and Eve sinned, all people (except Jesus) have been born paying attention to the wrong things and disobeying God (Romans 1:18–23).

   c. **Redemption:**

      Jesus always paid attention to God (John 8:28–29).

      Jesus always followed God's directions.

      Jesus died to take the punishment for sinners who don't pay attention to God and follow God's directions (Isaiah 53:6).

Those who believe in Jesus live in new ways (1 Peter 2:24).

Joined with Jesus, Christians can pay attention to God and follow God's directions (Romans 6).

Christians begin feasting with Christ as they enjoy him now (Revelation 3:20).

d. **Consummation:**

Read and discuss Revelation 19:6–9. Explain that Christians will celebrate Jesus at the best party in heaven forever.

Read Revelation 2:7b. Explain that people who are joined with Jesus enjoy the fruit of the tree of life.

5. At the end of the discussion, ask the children if it was difficult to pay attention. Discuss the reason(s) for that difficulty. Ask the children what they must *not* pay attention to (such as the treats on the tree), in order to pay attention to God's Word.

6. Thank God for Jesus and the way his obedience makes it possible for us to enjoy the greatest celebration forever. Thank God that Jesus' obedience makes it possible for us to begin enjoying God now. Then enjoy the treats together.

Options:

This activity may be done in several sittings, giving the children more opportunities to practice self-control as they wait for the treats on the tree.

Review:

When the children sin, help them confess their sin and seek God's forgiveness. Thank God that Jesus died for those who yield to temptation. Thank God that Jesus resisted temptation and gives us power to resist temptation.

Notes

Section 4

Pictures to Show

Instructions for Pictures to Show

• **Section 4: Pictures to Show** contains full-size Pictures 1–14 on pages 257–283. These pictures can be shown directly to the children.

• The required picture number and its location are indicated in the *Materials* box at the top right of each Lesson-opener page.

Note: When a picture is used in more than one lesson, the lesson numbers and page numbers are indicated on the lower right corner of the picture page.

Picture-1
Traffic Light

Picture-3
Construction Workers

Picture-5
Bear in the Zoo

Play-
Dough
Play-
Dough
Father, help me live by your Spirit as the new person you made me to be

Dirty Bag's Record of Sin

I did not honor God.	92,768 TIMES
I was not thankful.	309,227 TIMES
I complained.	1,692 TIMES
I loved something more than God.	7,395 TIMES
I coveted.	870 TIMES
I was malicious.	642 TIMES
I was mean.	1,989 TIMES
I lied.	472 TIMES
I gossiped.	513 TIMES
I boasted.	1,287 TIMES
I disobeyed my mom, dad, grandparent, teacher, or babysitter.	1,597 TIMES
I criticized people.	716 TIMES
I did not worship God.	172,506 TIMES
I did not love people.	2,963 TIMES
I was not respectful.	1,013 TIMES
I took something that was not mine.	67 TIMES
I argued, pouted, clammed up, blew up.	964 TIMES

Jesus' Record of Sin

I did not honor God.	______ TIMES
I was not thankful.	______ TIMES
I complained.	______ TIMES
I loved something more than God.	______ TIMES
I coveted.	______ TIMES
I was malicious.	______ TIMES
I was mean.	______ TIMES
I lied.	______ TIMES
I gossiped.	______ TIMES
I boasted.	______ TIMES
I disobeyed my mom, dad, grandparent, teacher, or babysitter.	______ TIMES
I criticized people.	______ TIMES
I did not worship God.	______ TIMES
I did not love people.	______ TIMES
I was not respectful.	______ TIMES
I took something that was not mine.	______ TIMES
I argued, pouted, clammed up, blew up.	______ TIMES

Section 5

Pictures to Download

Instructions for Pictures to Download

• **Section 5: Pictures to Download** contains Pictures 15–37 in miniature on pages 287–288. These miniature images refer to full-size pictures that can be downloaded, printed, and given to the children. The pictures are available at:

www.shepherdpress.com/moving-targets

• The required picture number and its location are indicated in the *Materials* box at the top right of each Lesson-opener page.

Note: Some pictures are used in more than one lesson, such as Picture-15, Picture-16, Picture-20, and Picture-21. The lesson numbers that correspond to the pictures are indicated beneath the miniature images on pages 287-288.